Healing a Broken Ma
one woman's determir
for Christ and her far
tive life in the kingdom. Despite overwhelming obstacles, Deborah Ross stayed the course, fought the fight, and her dream of a godly husband is now a living example of the saving grace of a loving God.

—JONI LAMB
COFOUNDER, DAYSTAR TELEVISION NETWORK

I was checking out your Web site. I love your heart, spirit, and ministry.

—ALVIN SLAUGHTER
CHRISTIAN RECORDING ARTIST

This woman is very good. Her teachings are spiritual, scriptural, and convicting!

—MELISSA PRINCE
THE INSPIRATION NETWORK (INSP)

When you sing, others can truly see how much you love the Lord!

—KATHRYN GOODING

I cried as I saw your testimony on the DVD even though I had heard it already! Thank you! It gives me hope and much encouragement to keep standing strong! Thank you! I need that very much! You are truly a blessing to me, Deborah!

—BEVERLY FERGUSON

I recommend Deborah wholeheartedly to anyone who is interested in hosting a Bible teacher and anointed singer who will inevitably lovingly confront this culture with the truth of God's Word.

—REV. MIKE WHITSON
FIRST BAPTIST CHURCH
INDIAN TRAIL, NC

I so loved your CD that you sent to me. God has anointed you to bless families and marriages. I want to encourage you today to keep going with your calling and vision to set the captives free! I'll never forget you introducing me to the Holy Ghost in your van that day. Your passion and fervor for the Lord will be mightily used. I love you.

—CHERYL HEBERT CUTLIP
PROJECT DANCE
NEW YORK

Your book is awesome! I am so thrilled to be a part of your Bible study!

—TERRY CONNELL-DAVIS
REAL ESTATE AGENT
MONROE, NC

Hello, Deborah, Thank you for wonderful teachings you are sending me. They are so good for all—men and women. I am planning to start an interdenominational study in my rural area to share them with my neighboring churches.

—PASTOR KHAEMBA MESHACK
BUNGOMA, KENYA

She ministers to the wounded and the broken-hearted. Her gifts and talents have been used by God for many years to bring encouragement to the downtrodden, a voice to the helpless, and renewed hope to the hope-less. Her writing style is direct and to the point.

—REV. AL LEWIS JR.
EXECUTIVE DIRECTOR
SAFER COMMUNITIES MINISTRY

Her writing is full of truth, love, and life-transforming revelation! Deborah Ross is a living testimony of God's grace and power! She is a mighty woman of God.

—LISA COLON, FOUNDER OF WEUSED2BU MINISTRIES

HEALING

a

BROKEN

MARRIAGE

DEBORAH ROSS

CREATION
HOUSE

HEALING A BROKEN MARRIAGE by Deborah Ross
Published by Creation House
A Charisma Media Company
600 Rinehart Road
Lake Mary, Florida 32746
www.charismamedia.com

Unless otherwise noted, all Scripture quotations are from the King James Version of the Bible.

Design Director: Bill Johnson
Cover design by Nathan Morgan

Library of Congress Control Number: 2010926533
International Standard Book Number: 978-1-61638-169-1

11 12 13 14 — 9 8 7 6 5 4 3
Printed in the United States of America

To my beautiful mother, Judy, who has taught me
to be strong and of good courage.

To my grandmother, Gimmama, who in all of her
ways exemplifies Christ.

To my friend Wendy, who has been instrumental
in the completion of this book.

To my boys, Preston and Garrett, my love for you
and my desire to see God use you in a powerful
way gave me the determination to persevere. I
pray you will be able to do even greater things
than your dad and I because of the generational
blessing you now live in.

To my wonderful husband, Jay, who has cheered
me on throughout the process of bringing this
book into the hands of many hurting families.
I love you!

To every relative, friend, and acquaintance, may
Jesus Christ make Himself more real to you
through my testimony.

To those I call my "team," thank you for your
sweet friendship, your professional help,
your unrelenting encouragement, and your
determination to promote the kingdom of God
through my testimony. Each one of you is a
precious treasure in my life.

To God be the glory!

CONTENTS

FOREWORD

I N A GENERATION of "throwaway marriages," it is refreshing to come across a marriage that has been salvaged through the faithful commitment to the wedding vows made before Holy God. In *Healing a Broken Marriage* you will discover how the Lord used a wife's trust in Holy God to bring her husband to repentance and produce a wonderful example of a Christ-like home.

The Lord has granted me the privilege of shepherding this couple for a number of years. I watched as life took them to the brink of divorce and then witnessed our Lord honor His Blessed Word when He spiritually made new a husband because of the promise of 1 Peter 3. Today this husband serves as a warrior on the front lines with me in ministry. His love and devotion to his wife and family are unquestioned. All because a wife dared to believe God and take Him at His Word.

Don't be intimidated by the graphic descriptions of this relationship. Don't be judgmental of the writer's approach. She dared, and God delivered, and now she is so bold as to share intimate details of her struggle and God's saving with the world.

Please know and understand that the same God who brought Deborah and Jay into oneness with Him can and will do the same for you. Read this not only for the pure pleasure of seeing the victory that God brought but also with great anticipation that He can do the same for you.

—REV. MIKE WHITSON
SENIOR PASTOR, FIRST BAPTIST CHURCH
OF INDIAN TRAIL, NORTH CAROLINA
WWW.FBCIT.ORG

INTRODUCTION

Preparation for Victory

H AVE YOU EVER wondered if you married the wrong guy? When you were a little girl, did you ever dream of living happily ever after with your handsome, compassionate, and loving prince? Did you think once you became born-again, that your husband would *quickly* see the difference Christ has made in your life and repent, only to be let down by his indifference to the need for this great salvation? Are you the breadwinner, spiritual leader, financial advisor, wife, mother, and—by far—the more responsible caregiver for the well being of your household? Is your spouse an alcoholic? Does your spouse have any addictive problems? What about pornography? Has your spouse ever been unfaithful?

If you have answered "yes" to any of these questions, this book was written with heartfelt wisdom, biblical knowledge, and experience just for you! In the book of Revelation (chapter 12, verse 11) we are taught that we "overcome the devil by the blood of the lamb, and by the word of our testimony." It is my prayer that the Lord will use my testimony to give you hope in what may seem to be a hopeless situation. This book is not another fluffy Bible study of "how to" but rather a lay it on the line transparent testimony and radical challenge for you to consider in being God's chosen woman for such a time as this (Esther 4:14)!

In this introduction, I have listed eight important action steps that need to be fulfilled in your preparation for victory. I believe these eight points are crucial in the journey of an overcomer. Read through each of these warrior attributes *very slowly* to fully digest the significance of what is being said. Once you have committed to clothing yourself according to these eight declarations, you will be ready to experience my story, receiving an impartation of my faith in God's Word.

ACTION NO. 1: SALVATION

Marvel not that I said unto thee, Ye must be born again.
—JOHN 3:7

John 3:3 tells us, "Except a man [or woman] is born again, he [or she] cannot see the kingdom of God." Every restoration principle revealed in this book is established in the kingdom of God. If you truly expect to benefit from reading *Healing a Broken Marriage: Love Never Fails,* first and foremost, *you* must be born again! The Bible says in Romans 10:9, if we confess with our mouth and believe in our hearts that Jesus is Lord, we shall be saved!

If you are not a born-again child of God, I want to encourage you to turn to page 161 in the back of this book for instructions on how to become a Christian. Do it now!

If you *are* a born-again Christian, but you have slipped from your walk with the Lord, stop and pray now. Offer up a heart of repentance to your heavenly Father before you read this book. Don't let anything hinder you from receiving all of the benefits from the life-changing principles that are taught throughout these pages.

Moving forward, let's examine the word *salvation.* In both the Hebrew and Greek translations, the word *salvation* means so much more than a ticket to heaven. In fact, the word *salvation* means: "deliverance, health, welfare, aid, victory, prosperity, rescue, defend, liberty, to be safe and to preserve." God wants you and your family made whole; not only in the life to come, but in your life on Earth, as well. Let this comforting characteristic of God sink down in your spirit so your faith can rest in God's good plans for your life.

Have you *really* been able to cast your care—your marriage—upon the Lord, because He cares for you (1 Peter 5:7)? Do you really "trust" the Lord to give you the desires of your heart?

> *Delight thyself also in the* Lord: *and he shall give thee the desires of thine heart.*
> —Psalm 37:4

Action No. 2: Read

Building a trust relationship with the Lord will require you to put practical Bible reading into action. Notice I said, "Bible reading." I did not say that you should read inspirational books or work through a lot of Bible study guides. While there is nothing wrong with Bible study guides and inspirational books in moderation, I believe the only true way to build an "intimate relationship" with God—a relationship full of faith that will believe Him for a miracle—is to go straight to the source... the Bible!

> *In the beginning was the Word, and the Word was with God, and the* **Word was God**.
> —John 1:1, emphasis added

Our Bible says that the Word *is* God. They are the same. This means, every time you read your Bible, you are actually reading God! That's powerful!

As you read God's Word, faith will rise up inside of you. Of course, the devil will come right behind those liberating promises you receive from God's Word, chanting, "It won't work for you. Your marriage is hopeless. Your spouse will never change." *The devil is a liar!* Just keep reading God's Word and meditating on His promises. Soon the voice of the Holy Spirit will ring louder than the voice of the devil and you will begin to walk through these tough times with a heart of hope instead of despair.

Remember, it only takes a very small amount of faith to believe God for a miracle. The Bible calls it "mustard seed faith." But Jesus tells us that we can move mountains with our mustard seed faith (Matthew 17:20)! If you have some mountains that need to be moved in your marriage, read your Bible daily to strengthen your faith.

> *For verily I say unto you, If ye have faith as a grain of mustard seed, ye shall say unto this mountain, Remove hence to yonder place; and it shall remove;* **and nothing shall be impossible unto you.**
> —MATTHEW 17:20, EMPHASIS ADDED

ACTION NO. 3: PRAY

Have you ever heard the cliché, "Prayer changes things"? Well, it does! My situation did not turn around by chance. I believe God answered my prayers because I sought Him daily for strength to endure—and power to overcome.

This book has a lot to say about prayer. It is imperative that you grab hold of the importance of a steady prayer life. Once your prayer life is grounded and rooted in God's love for you and your family, no demon force in hell can stop God's blessings from rushing in to restore your home. This horrendous battle can only be won on your knees; so, get ready to do mighty warfare, conquering the powers of darkness—from a kneeling position.

> *Finally, my brethren, be strong in the Lord, and in the power of his might. Put on the whole armour of God, that ye may be able to stand against the wiles of the devil. For we wrestle not against flesh and blood, but against principalities, against powers, against the rulers of the darkness of this world, against spiritual wicked-ness in high places...And take the helmet of salvation, and the sword of the Spirit, which is the word of God:* **Praying always** *with all prayer and supplication in the Spirit, and watching thereunto with all perseverance and supplication for all saints.*
> —EPHESIANS 6:10–11; 17–18, EMPHASIS ADDED

ACTION NO. 4: SURROUND YOURSELF

> *Iron sharpeneth iron; so a man sharpeneth the counte-nance of his friend.*
> —PROVERBS 27:17

Surround yourself with fire-baptized Christian people *who believe in the supernatural power of God!* I have found that not everyone professing to be a Christian really believes the prom-ises of God, when it comes to a crisis situation. It may be hard to find more than one or two true "faith warriors" that will believe with you in your situation. Whatever you do, close your ears to the naysayer!

Satan will try his best to "set you up" with ungodly advice from all directions. He'll even attempt to use Christians to discourage you. You must develop a keen sense of discernment and avoid unscriptural "words" from penetrating your soul.

I put my spiritual "wet suit" on everyday. The Bible calls this the shield of faith. Whenever words of discouragement come my way, I repel them in my spirit man. Never acting ugly to others who offer unscriptural advice, I simply avoid keeping company with these people in the future. Many of these well-meaning souls simply don't know what to say. It reminds me of Job's friends. Like Job, we must forgive them, but we don't have to listen to them.

Don't meditate on negative words. Seek out radical Christian friends to believe with you in your journey for a miracle. The Lord is always faithful to bring these types of people in your path, so watch for them.

ACTION NO. 5: ATTEND CHURCH

Not forsaking the assembling of ourselves together, as the manner of some is; but exhorting one another: and so much the more, as ye see the day approaching.
—HEBREWS 10:25

So often people will say they don't need to go to church in order to be a Christian. While this is true in theory, it is not the way God intended for His children to live. Attending church regularly will keep you in fellowship with people that will love you and support your cause—your marriage.

Going to church each week keeps you focused on God and not on your circumstances. Jesus knew what He was doing when he established the church. Don't let excuses rob you from attending church regularly.

Be sure that you are involved in a loving church that preaches the full truth of the Word of God. Your church should help you grow in your faith!

ACTION NO. 6: DEVELOP YOUR FRUIT

And be not conformed to this world: but be ye trans-formed by the renewing of your mind, that ye may prove what is that good, and acceptable, and perfect, will of God.

—ROMANS 12:2

To acquire a marked posture for triumph, you must work on developing your personal "fruit of the spirit" as found in Galatians 5:22–23. In this passage, we are taught that love, joy, peace, longsuffering, gentleness, goodness, faith, meekness, and temperance are all fruit that should show forth in a believer's life. *That means in the good times and the bad!* I recommend that you start right now praying the Lord will help you to love your husband with the love of Jesus—even though he may not seem so lovable at the present time. Ask God to keep you passionate about your spouse. Ask Him to strengthen you so that you can be a lover to your husband, even at the most undesirable of times. *Cry out in prayer, "Lord, keep me in love with my husband!"*

On page 159 of this book, you'll find a beautiful "marriage prayer" designed to help you stay focused on your role in the restoration of your marriage.

ACTION NO. 7: CHOOSE TO BE A WINNER

I call heaven and earth to record this day against you, that I have set before you life and death, blessing and cursing: therefore choose life, that both thou and thy seed may live.

—DEUTERONOMY 30:19

In this passage, God sets before us life and death, blessing and cursing; but he commands us to choose life, if we want to live and see our families live. You must make a choice right now to move forward by believing God's Word against all odds. Do not look back. Don't doubt. Don't think of what "should have been" or "could have been." Instead, meditate on what God's Word says "will be." The scriptures tell us plainly that pressing onward is what qualifies us to experience kingdom benefits.

No man [or woman], having put his hand to the plough, and looking back, is fit for the kingdom of God.

—LUKE 9:62

Choose to be more than a conqueror through Christ who strengthens you (Romans 8:37)! God gives us a choice in this war that rages all around. Yes, He gives us a choice, but He also prompts us to choose the path that leads to His incredible blessing. This path is not always the easiest; even so, God's Word promises that we have the mastery in every situation according to His will. Marriage *is* His will! *Make a choice now to fight the good fight of faith in order to receive the salvation of the Lord for the sake of everyone in your household.*

ACTION NO. 8: TRUST YOUR DADDY, ABBA FATHER

> *But without faith it is impossible to please him: for he that cometh to God must believe that he is, and that **he is a rewarder of them that diligently seek him.***
>
> —HEBREWS 11:6, EMPHASIS ADDED

Trusting in God's love for you is essential to receiving the victory and breaking the generational curse that is seeking to destroy your marriage, your dreams, and hopes for the future. Perhaps you both were lost when you first married. Maybe you knew your mate was lost but you married him anyway. Or, maybe you thought your husband was saved, but now you're just not sure anymore. Regardless of your circumstance, the Lord wants to *restore* what the canker worm and the locust have eaten (Joel 2:25).

Your job now is to "stand strong" upon God's promises and follow the leading of the Holy Spirit in *each crisis.* The Lord loves you, your husband, and your children. He wants to heal all aspects of your marriage. Don't give up! The best things in life will cost you something, and this could be one of the most mentally, physically, and spiritually expensive prices you'll ever have to pay. But, let me tell you now that "eye has not seen and ear has not heard the [wonderful] things that God has in store for those that believe" (1 Corinthians 2:9). I am living proof of the goodness of God concerning His will for your family to be made whole. Now get ready to walk with me through my journey of faith; one that has brought me from the dungeons of despair to the glorious castles of abundant life. God is no respecter of persons. What He did for me, He will do for you. Just believe!

Many waters cannot quench love, neither can the floods drown it.

—SONG OF SOLOMON 8:7

one

UNEQUALLY YOKED

Life Lessons

> • God's Word is full of "keys" that open doors to the treasures of life.
> • We must diligently search God's Word for answers to life's most perplexing questions—if we expect to be victorious warriors in God's kingdom.
> • The Holy Spirit will reveal hidden truths that can only be understood by those whose hearts have been purified by the precious blood of Jesus.

And he said, unto you it is given to know the
mysteries of the kingdom of God: but to others
in parables; that seeing they might not see,
and hearing they might not understand.

—LUKE 8:10

BEFORE I TAKE you down my life's road, I'd like to illuminate a few things that will help you understand the heart of my story. In these upcoming pages, I

have raised the windows of my soul, revealing deep reflec-
tive thoughts that I pondered throughout each season of my
Christian growth. You will journey with me from my wedding
day vows up through the present. As every life experience has
been tearfully and joyfully relived, I have carefully scripted my
commitment of holding onto God's Word for my miracle—a
born-again husband and a peaceful Christian home.

I will be sharing some very personal frustrations that include
details from my husband's "old nature." I have done so in an
effort to help you realize the magnitude of God's redemptive
power. If He can change my husband, He can certainly change
yours, too! Nothing is too hard for Him (Jeremiah 32:17).

Carefully woven throughout my "marriage story" are the
many struggles I have faced in understanding the organized
church. As a growing Christian, it seemed each time my faith
would take flight, it would spiral back into a state of confusion,
as Christian leaders on every side doubted and disagreed over
the awesome promises I was reading about in God's Word. I
believe God will use this transparent discloser of my personal
search for answers to help you grasp the importance of going
beyond status quo. If you want to experience God's best, you
must press on. You must dive in deep.

> *But this one thing I do, forgetting those things which are*
> *behind, and reaching forth unto those things which are*
> *before, I press toward the mark for the prize of the high*
> *calling of God in Christ Jesus.*
>
> —PHILIPPIANS 3:13

It is also with great joy that I affirm my husband as being
everything and more than I could ever ask God for. According

to Ephesians 3:20, the Lord actually did "exceedingly and abundantly above all" I could have ever asked or thought in restoring our marriage. He even changed the desires of my husband's mind and heart. Now, I am married to my knight in shining armor: a man of God who is full of vision and purpose for our family. Even though the road to marital bliss started out much differently for us, God is faithful and His Word is true!

> *Now unto him that is able to do exceeding abundantly above all that we ask or think, according to the power that worketh in us, Unto him be glory in the church by Christ Jesus throughout all ages, world without end. Amen.*
> —EPHESIANS 3:20–21

Here's my story...

When my husband and I met, dated, and then married in 1984, neither of us knew the Lord. Oh yes, we both believed in God (so do the demons who tremble at His name) but we had never made a commitment to follow Christ. We were not born again. And so, our marriage started out as many others do; that is, we both lived lives of selfish ambition. While we were very much in love, our relationship was more about "what my mate does for me" instead of "what I do for my mate." We were married on my husband's birthday, each of us twenty-two years of age.

At the time that we met, I owned and operated a very successful dance and modeling studio while my husband ran a pawnshop downtown for his dad. As a high energy and very competitive entrepreneur, I lived a life that was fast paced and very detail oriented. With a schedule that kept me working six and seven days per week, my days were long, consisting of both first and second shift hours. My husband's life was more laid back. His job was nine to five, affording him afternoons and evenings for more leisure activity.

Within the first few years of our marriage, my business rapidly expanded into three locations. I was promptly maturing into the role of an accomplished businesswoman; a woman of prestige in our community. Swiftly moving toward new heights of success, I adapted to managing an ever-increasing yearly flux of students, their parents, and a large staff. From the world's point of view we were doing G-R-E-A-T. We had lots of money, a nice new home, two new cars, and we were happy—so we thought—with our independent lives. I didn't mind being the breadwinner. I loved my job, and besides, making the most money allowed me to be "in control" of getting what I wanted, when I wanted it. Isn't that what we are all told will bring happiness?

Well, it wasn't long until money, power, and things eventually failed to fill the gap in my restless soul. At the age of twenty-seven, I began to search for life's meaning. My spirit yearned, "Surely there is more to happiness in this world than what I am experiencing." Not knowing where to start and being tainted by a whirlwind of advice from this world, I read new age books, tried healing rocks and crystals, and even prayed to Jesus (a God I did not know). Thankfully, because of God's all-knowing (omniscient) great love of mercy and grace, He heard my cries. The sovereign, one true God of the universe, came to my rescue, surrounding me with Christian people who officially introduced me to this Jesus I had heard so much about as a child.

Finally! After nearly a year of exploring the various ways of finding inner peace, I fully surrendered to the wooing of the Holy Spirit, repenting of my sinful lifestyle and making a commitment in my heart to follow Jesus. After all, He was the one I had always believed to be the Son of God—"the way, the truth, and the life" (John 14:6). My appointed time had come to take a leap of faith; to take action toward being who God designed me to be.

As I made my way down the aisle of that small Baptist church one Sunday morning, I could almost hear the chains that had kept me bound for so long as they crumbled to the floor. Not knowing what to say, other than, "I want to be saved," the preacher gently led me in a beautiful prayer, sealing my decision to follow Christ Jesus. At that moment, something supernatural took place in my spirit and I was forever changed. For the first time in my life my eyes were opened! The world appeared more colorful and alive than I ever remembered! My heart was leaping with joy and my soul was at peace! On top of that, I was pleasantly surprised to read my Bible and actually understand the scriptures! Even more astonishing, I found people "noticed" I was different, just by my countenance!

Suddenly, my heart longed to live a holy life. I wanted to learn as much as I could about God's Word. I was born again! Hallelujah! Shortly after, in obedience to God's Word, I followed in water baptism.

> *Therefore if any man be in Christ, he is a new creature: old things are passed away; behold, all things are become new.*
> —2 CORINTHIANS 5:17

Now for some reason, the Lord chose to introduce me—a Baptist girl by tradition—to spiritual gifts and the supernatural power of living in His kingdom, right off the bat. I am one of those "seeing-is-believing" kind of people, and the Lord knew exactly what I needed to soar in my faith. Early on in my new Christian walk, I was invited to Women's Aglow meetings and nondenominational church services by Christians the Lord strategically brought into my life. It was the teachings of those Charismatic or Pentecostal believers that helped me connect the dots in my search for spiritual understanding of "God with us." I wanted ALL of what God had for me! I was determined to investigate the validity of these testimonies, teachings, and manifestations of the Holy Spirit—all coming forth from these radical believers.

Initially, I did not understand everything I saw and heard. But, as I earnestly asked God to personally reveal to me—through His Word—His will on the matter; I was convinced that everything—from tongues, to healing, to miracles—was of God. Interestingly, during this same season of my life, our Baptist church offered a study by Henry Blackaby called "Experiencing God." This study further confirmed to me the realm of the supernatural that God desires for His children to live in. All of this was so new and amazing to me!

Now the "gifts of the Spirit" were of particular interest. It seemed everyone I observed operating in these gifts was also "baptized in the Holy Spirit" with evidence of praying in an unknown tongue. I wanted to be used of the Lord in this way, so I began to seek understanding from the scriptures on this matter. For months, I studied the books of Acts and Corinthians, carefully underlining scriptures that pointed to this phenomenon of "speaking in tongues." I would ask the Lord questions, and He would faithfully answer each one in His Word, further confirming to me this amazing gift and its relevance for the church today.

Since I did not want to be influenced by the "power of sugges-tion" concerning my personal receiving of tongues, I decided to sit in my great room (alone) to petition God for this gift. I prayed, "Lord, if praying in tongues is real, I want it, because I want all of You. If it is not real, then I will get away from these Pentecostal believers, because I do not want to be mixed up in any sort of cult or false doctrine." (I suppose I was still a little unsure in my faith, even though God had clearly confirmed this gift in His Word.)

Much to my surprise, as I began to worship the Lord, with my hands lifted high—something I had never done before—my mental babblings, which sounded like baby talk, took on a new dimension. I went from laughing at myself, thinking, "If anyone saw me they would think I was C-R-A-Z-Y," to inti-mately communing with God. The Lord touched me, and I began to flow in my prayer language!

> *For they heard them speak with tongues, and magnify God.*
>
> —ACTS 10:46

Wow! I'll be honest with you; it frightened me at first. I knew beyond the shadow of a doubt that the Mighty God of the universe just took me into the Holy of Holies. He was in the room with me and was intimately pouring His love over and through me in a way I had never experienced before. Thank goodness the Holy Spirit is a gentleman who does not force worshipers to do anything they are not comfortable with. I quickly stopped praying in an unknown tongue and sat in awe at what had just taken place...

Not many days following, while at a Pentecostal church

service, the pastor gave an altar call for people to come forward and have hands laid on them for receiving their prayer language. Eagerly, I went forward. As a precious woman of God prayed over me, my new language flowed forth like rivers of living water (John 7:38). I was not afraid! It was wonderful! At this same moment, the Lord gave me a belly full of joy and bones full of fire that was almost uncontainable (Jeremiah 20:9). I was transformed even beyond my initial salvation experience. Wow! Wow! Wow!

> *And they were all filled with the Holy Ghost, and began to speak with other tongues, as the spirit gave them utterance.*
>
> —ACTS 2:4

Following my conversion experience, I couldn't wait to introduce my husband to the Redeemer of my soul, my precious Jesus, who healed me of all my emotional pain!

You see, my parents divorced when I was only nine years old. Staggered memories of the years before their divorce proved empty and uncertain for a little girl who watched her family slowly fall apart. I grew to feel abnormal, like a throwaway child. My childhood thoughts were, "Why didn't my daddy and mommy love me enough to stay together? Why did my family have to be deformed?" A part of me felt special, as if I were born for a purpose; but another part of me felt hopeless, as if things would never turn out the way I had dreamt.

Up until the time of my salvation, I spent my days trying to make my own way in this world. Thinking I had been dealt a very unfair hand in this game of life, Satan managed to keep me feeling insignificant and detached from reality for nearly twenty-eight years. In an effort to make myself feel loved and accepted, I sank myself into my career. As long as I could please people, achieve another award, or make more money than the year before, I was satisfied—at least, until time for the next fix. Like a drug addict, I craved success, accolades, and man's approval daily. My career had become my god and in a sense, "I" had become my own god, as well.

Praise the Lord, at the moment of my salvation, Jesus settled my heart and gave me a peace I had never known before. On top of that, my conversion was a lot like Saul who became Paul. Whether masquerading as a sinner or crusading as a saint, my personality thrives on being the leader of the pack. As one who was radically transformed, I literally wanted to get on top of housetops and shout to the world about my awesome new life in Christ. I couldn't believe that anyone would ever reject something so wonderful as God's love and forgiveness. Feeling as though this great salvation had somehow been kept a secret from me all these years, I didn't want anyone else to live in the dark unnecessarily, as I had.

When I shared my marvelous born-again experience with my best friend (my husband) I just knew he would instantly say, "I want to know this Jesus, too!" Unfortunately, this was not the case, at all. You see, my husband had also come from a broken home, and he would have many obstacles in his mind to overcome before he would buy into the born-again experience. Secretly, his adulthood was haunted by childhood memories that traumatized his innocence. Attempting to help raise his little brother and sister, my husband's caregivers took drunken binges, oftentimes lasting a week or more. My husband grew up fast, but not whole. As a grown man he looked real good on the outside, but inside he was a little boy searching for peace.

When I shared my new faith in Jesus with my husband, his shocking response was, "Oh yes, I got baptized when I was thirteen." As a new Christian, this was very confusing to me. By this time, we had been married for six years already and he had never mentioned having a relationship with Jesus. I had never seen him read the Bible. We didn't attend church regularly as a couple. And even more perplexing, we both had been accustomed to "partying" on the weekends. He never showed any concern over being convicted of sinning against God. I was so disappointed that my newfound faith was not as exciting for my husband as it was for me.

At first, I was so "high" in my walk with Jesus that I didn't dwell on my husband's lack of excitement. As a baby Christian, I didn't have a complete understanding of the fruit that should have been evident in my husband's life if he were truly a born-again child of God. After all, my husband was very convincing that he had become a Christian as a young teenager, and he believed what he was saying—or at least he appeared to believe what he was saying. "Maybe he had a different way of expressing his salvation? Maybe he was backslidden? Maybe he hadn't grown in Christ as fast as I had? Maybe his conversion was a slow process—unlike my life-changing born-again experience?" I was getting unscriptural advice from every direction, further muddling my perception of how to pray for my spouse. I was so confused.

I know thy works, that thou art neither cold nor hot: I would thou wert cold or hot. So because thou art luke-

*warm, and neither cold nor hot, I will spue thee out of
my mouth.*
—REVELATION 3:15–16

Now don't misunderstand me, I did talk openly about the
things I was learning from God's Word to my husband. While I
tried to remain even-tempered and understanding throughout his
many objections and lack of hunger for the things of God, I must
admit, in the early part of my salvation walk, there were times I
completely lost my cool. Once, in a shouting match of passionate
preaching that was meant for the pulpit and not the home, I told
my husband he was "on a bobsled to hell." I don't recommend
trying to beat the Word of God into your mate with scare tactics
and over-the-top drills. This can backfire. You can actually push
your mate further from you and the Lord. What I am saying is
that I was not perfect in my quest to see my husband become a
man of God. More than anything, I desired to do whatever God
required to bring about salvation for my family. I learned very
quickly that the only way to do this was to keep His Word before
my eyes; and, to keep His Word deep within my heart!

*Thy word have I hid in mine heart, that I may not sin
against thee.*
—PSALM 119:11

Over time, the closer I got to Jesus, the more I began to
notice my husband was actually threatened by my devotion to
becoming all that God wanted me to be. Strangely, at times, I
think he was flat-out jealous over my relationship with Jesus.

Insisting on taking me to nightclubs and social events I
didn't care to attend, always stopping to buy beer, in hopes I
would want to join him in this festive night out on the town,

his favorite ploy was to buy me a wine cooler. He justified that I would enjoy drinking it with him because, after all, these wine coolers had a much lower alcohol content than beer. It would aggravate him if I did not want to participate in having a "little drink." Our compatible relationship suddenly rubbed with sparks of friction. I wanted to live holy; he wanted to live worldly. We were on opposite ends of the spectrum when it came to our definition of fun. The Lord would have to teach me how to be a wife that could go along with her husband's plans and yet remain godly.

And so, my charge, as a wife who longed to be able to share these wonderful revelations of truth from God's Word with the man I loved, began. I had no idea of what the next *twelve years* would bring as I grew in Christ; all the while, married to a man who was determined to maintain his *counterfeit stance of salvation*. Always eager to point out to me his "nobody's perfect" philosophy and his "family heritage theology," he was convinced he had what I had, based upon the fact that he had been baptized and made a church member at an earlier age. Only time would reveal to both of us the parable of how souls are compared to wheat and tares.

> *And he spake many things unto them in parables, saying, Behold, a sower went forth to sow; And when he sowed, some seeds fell by the way side, and the fowls came and devoured them up: Some fell upon stony places, where they had not much earth: and forthwith they sprung up, because they had not deepness of earth: And when the sun was up, they were scorched; and because they had no root, they withered away. And some fell among thorns; and the thorns sprung up, and choked them: But*

other fell into good ground, and brought forth fruit, some an hundredfold, some sixtyfold, some thirtyfold...Hear ye therefore the parable of the sower.

—MATTHEW 13:3–6, 18

LIFE APPLICATION

If you are struggling to understand the spiritual condition of your husband, so that you can effectively pray for him, read the entire chapter of Matthew 13. Ask God to reveal to you the man behind the mask—the soul of your husband.

two

GROWING IN CHRIST

LIFE LESSONS

- In order to effectively pray for your spouse, you will need to come to terms with the "root" of the problem.
- Finding the root will involve peeling away layers of masks: things normally "swept under the rug," excuses, preconceived ideas, and even denominational theologies that have hindered your ability to see things through the eyes of God.
- As you pull down these strongholds, your understanding will be enlightened, creating a flow of prayer that is honest and unwavering.

*If any of you lack wisdom, let him ask of God, that giveth to all men liberally, and upbraideth not; and it shall be given him. But let him ask in faith, **not wavering**. For he that wavereth is like a wave of the sea driven with the wind and tossed.*

—JAMES 1:5–6, EMPHASIS ADDED

WITHIN THE NEXT four years following my salvation experience, my husband and I gave birth to two beautiful baby boys. Our lives as a married couple now took on an even deeper meaning as we shared our responsibilities, our love, and our hopes through the lives of our children. For me, this was all the more reason to live for Christ, to make every moment count. My husband was glad that I had chosen to live for Christ—for our children's sake. Deep in his heart, he knew it was right. Nevertheless, he refused to take responsibility in leading our family—as a man of God. Shrinking into Satan's cunning deception, my husband accepted the back seat position of spiritual leadership.

My husband has always been a good man. With a tender heart that easily overflowed with nurturing paternal love, I felt his parenting skills often seemed better than mine. He was so natural at juggling our new lives as working parents. Ready in an instant to relax and have fun with our boys, nothing threw him. I, on the other hand, felt the pressure of our daily obligations. I was the more serious one. It would horrify me to come home from work only to find my husband had strapped our infant onto his back, loaded up our two year old, and headed out the door with his football buddy to press through the crowds at the Panthers Stadium, downtown Charlotte. I could not believe that he had the nerve to take our babies into this type of atmosphere, especially as a solo act. Even worse, he would sip a few beers along the way. His parenting skills were great, but his lack of good judgment kept my emotions on edge.

When it came to church, he went every Sunday morning. Now, he never felt the desire to go with us on Sunday nights, and he certainly would not consider going on Wednesdays. He thought that he had done his part for the week and concluded that God was proud of him for his efforts. Consequently, when it came to living out Christ before our children, it was "whatever mother says goes." I quickly became the spiritual leader of the house. This was my new title—added onto all of the others: entrepreneur and breadwinner, wife, mother, financial advisor, maid, cook, and over-all "the more responsible caretaker of the home."

Week after week, my hope was deferred. The preacher did his best to call sinners to repentance, but my husband never budged. Left to face yet another week of anticipated bad fruit from his life, it befuddled me how we managed to hear two different gospels from the words of one sermon.

Gambling, drinking, drugs, pornography (he thought I didn't know about), hanging out with sinners, and deception were just some of the bad fruit that would randomly surface each week. My husband was a professional liar (which I now know is a characteristic of all people controlled by demons). He was so good at it, I usually believed him: I took the bait—hook, line, and sinker. For instance, so many times it would be obvious he was intoxicated to the point of being flat-out drunk; still he somehow managed to cause me to question my perception, by assuring me he only had two beers. Then there were those occasions when I found pot seeds in his car, but he "didn't know where they came from." He became so good at fabricating lies, I think he actually began to believe his own bunk.

I felt in my heart that my husband couldn't be born again. How could a born-again person continually do these things? After all, some of his sinful behavior patterns were the very things that Jesus had just saved me from. If being born-again caused me to hate my old sinful nature, it only made sense that my husband should hate his sinful life—if he were truly a child of God. While

I wouldn't say he really liked his sinful lifestyle, he certainly made no efforts toward changing it. Holding his head high on Sunday mornings—as if he were a pillar of the church—he was faithful to attend each and every Sunday morning. The Bible does say that pride will cause a man to be brought down, and I was fearful my husband was setting himself up for a big fall.

> *Pride goeth before destruction, and an haughty spirit before a fall.*
>
> —PROVERBS 16:18

True believers are known by their fruits, but because I did see "some" good fruit (along with the bad) I didn't know what to believe. Plus, I was hoping for the best, which I would later learn was the most important thing for me to do. First Corinthians 13:7 says that love "hopes" all things, and I was hopelessly hopeful!

Unfortunately, in the process of my hoping, I was wavering in my prayers. I did not know "what" to pray for. Should I pray for his salvation, or should I pray for him to stop drinking and gambling? Was it right for me to question my husband's salvation in my prayer time with the Lord? Quite honestly, since I had never been married to a born-again "Christian man of God," I was a little apprehensive about how life would be if he were really upright in all of his ways. Subconsciously, I think I was afraid of giving up my role as spiritual leader. Or, maybe I just didn't feel worthy enough to be married to an all-out godly man.

> *Let us hold fast the profession of our faith without wavering; (for he is faithful that promised).*
>
> —HEBREWS 10:23

And so, days turned into months, and months turned into years as I desperately sought answers from God's Word concerning the condition of my husband's soul. Was there any hope for our future? Undeniably, the years that passed were not all bad. In fact, during our many years of being unequally yoked in marriage, we enjoyed some wonderful times together (at least, as far as we knew was possible up to this point in our relationship). In this case, ignorance of what could be was a good thing. I didn't know what I was missing so I was satisfied with receiving love from a man that didn't know how to love me as Christ loves the church (Ephesians 5:25). His carnal love was enough to keep me hoping for more.

> *Now faith is the substance of things hoped for, the evidence of things not seen.*
>
> —HEBREWS 11:1

Aside from our relationship as husband and wife, I was continuing to grow spiritually in my walk with the Lord. I joined the choir, taught Sunday school, and was renewing my mind with the Word of God daily. Meanwhile, my husband was spiritually progressing like a turtle! Sometimes taking one step forward but always falling two steps back—when you are a desperate wife, anything seems better than nothing at all. I took what I could get and remained in faith, believing my miracle was just around the corner.

The Lord kept me in the Baptist church for most of those twelve years while waiting—diligently praying—for my husband to come around. I must admit, after I received my prayer language, I did not want to stay in the Baptist church. I did not have anything against the Baptist church, but quickly found out that my testimony was going to have to stay a secret if I wanted to get plugged in where I was. You see, I innocently told my preacher about my new prayer language and how the Lord plunged me into the Holy Ghost fire. As a new believer, I was appalled—quite honestly, I was crushed—when he tried to convince me that praying in tongues was not for today, as he handed me a distinctively Baptist booklet to support his disapproval.

Didn't he know it was futile to tell a fire-baptized Christian to deny this blessed gift from the Lord? As my excitement was diminished to a sick feeling in my stomach, I decided that it was best for me to move on. I desperately wanted to be in a fellowship of like-minded believers where I could worship freely.

> *Quench not the Spirit.*
> —1 THESSALONIANS 5:19

My husband, on the other hand, was not at all interested in being around any supernatural move of the Holy Spirit. That was just too close to the fire for someone living in sin. He felt safe in our Baptist church, because it was easier for him to pretend without fear of some radical Pentecostal believer "reading his mail" with a "word of knowledge." The whole thought of praying in the spirit was frightening to my husband. He knew it was real. He had witnessed the difference my prayer language made in my Christian life. Fully believing my testimony and genuinely happy for me to have this gift, he just didn't want God to get a hold of him like that. I think he feared having to give up his many vices more than anything else. He did not want to change his ways.

I sought counsel about whether or not I should change churches. I wanted to leave my husband behind. He was poking along in his efforts to know God while I had an unquenchable hunger and thirst for more spiritual food from my Lord's table.

Disappointed, I was advised to continue attending church with my husband, providing it was a place of worship that taught the uncompromising gospel message of salvation, according to the Holy Bible.

Thankfully, my husband decided on his own to begin attending a different Baptist church that emanated a more charismatic worship style. They still did not talk about gifts of the spirit, miracles, prospering, or prophetic ministry—of any sort—favorably, but at least they were hungrier than the previous church we attended. I don't recall telling this preacher about my prayer language, but I do suspect he noticed something different about me. Praying the Lord would reveal truth about spiritual gifts to this church, I sat quietly and watched the Lord faithfully send Spirit-filled witnesses into our congregation. I can recall several times in which random questions or comments would be voiced during open forums at a week of revival meetings. These bold servants brought up controversial scriptures that didn't seem to line up with some of the denominational doctrines that were esteemed as final. The Lord was faithful to speak, but I'm sorry to report that His voice fell on deaf ears.

We stayed at that church for a couple of years. I like to think of our time there as a "stepping stone"—preparation for the next level the Lord would take us to as a family. I was ready to move-on-up, quickly, so to speak, but my husband needed to take baby steps in his understanding about the things of God. He was still unsaved, but slowly growing in curiosity about the different beliefs that Christians had.

It's too bad that Christians have to make the gospel so complicated with their man-made doctrines that divide and cause confusion among unbelievers. My husband couldn't understand why some churches lifted their hands in worship, while others thought it was strange to lift your hands. He couldn't understand why some Christians prayed in tongues, while others thought tongues were of the devil. He couldn't understand why some churches used a screen to display their words to the songs, while others used hymnbooks. He couldn't understand why some churches had padded pews and others had folding chairs. He couldn't understand why some churches taught prosperity, while others taught being poor was what God wanted. The biggest obstacle for him to overcome was why so many hypocrites were in the church. He couldn't see that he was the biggest hypocrite of them all!

Finally, we ended up at a very exciting, very loving, and fast-growing Baptist church that actually believed in anointing people with oil to be healed. This church did not have the same hang-ups about the supernatural power of God as the other two. While this church did not teach on praying in tongues and did not operate in any of the other spiritual gifts openly, there was a freedom of worship along with anointed preaching. The preacher at this church didn't try to hide behind mystical theology and cute little stories that left me hanging, wondering what I just heard. This church had a maturity I had not seen in the other two churches we were members of earlier.

The first time we ever attended this church, which was

much larger than the others we had come from, the preacher somehow spotted us out in the crowd, welcomed us, and then offered to take us out to dinner. On the way to the restaurant, my husband taunted, "Be sure and tell him about your prayer language." I firmly responded, "I'm not telling him anything—unless he asks." I had already been shot down trying to convince a Baptist preacher about my testimony, so I wasn't about to bring it up unless the Lord specifically opened the door to that aspect of conversation. Well, wouldn't you know it, that's just what the Lord did! Before I could comfortably get into my seat, that preacher looked me in the eyes and asked, "What made you turn your secular dance studio into a ministry?" This pastor had a curiosity to know what was different about me that would make me such a fanatic about Christ in my everyday life.

That night, I told my entire testimony. I shared my conversion experience and then told of how my faith was set on fire upon my baptism of the Holy Spirit. My husband listened intently and waited for this preacher's response. You see, my husband wasn't interested in our conversation about the Lord but rather preoccupied in the potential disagreement that we might have as two people claiming to know the Bible. This would help my husband to justify his doubt about the accuracy of the scriptures. He was playing the devil's advocate.

When I finished my testimony I was pleasantly surprised to hear that this Baptist preacher believed me. He was the first one I had met, up until this point, who believed in the supernatural power of God. This was very exciting for me! The Lord kept us at this church for about five years.

I must admit, since my husband would not go to church with me on Sunday nights or Wednesday nights, I would very often slip off to a local "Church of God" or nondenominational church meeting with a friend. I was faithful to serve in our Baptist church, teaching Sunday school and singing in the choir, but I still had a hunger to understand doctrinal differences between the two denominations. I wanted to know more about the Lord. We are never commanded to be complacent in our walk. If you are hungry for more, and your husband is not, don't die waiting on him to take you out to eat. There are ways to take baby steps with him and yet take giant steps for yourself, so seek to know all you can about the Lord now, before the battle gets any tougher! You'll need all of God's wisdom, knowledge, and understanding your soul can comprehend, if your situation gets worse before it gets better, as mine did.

During the next five years of attending this Baptist church, I am ashamed to tell you how my lost husband actually got involved. He became an assistant Sunday school teacher and even went as a chaperone on a youth retreat one summer. At this point, I was really confused about his salvation! He had gotten more skilled at hiding his sinful lifestyle so that a lot of what others saw was "works" for the Lord. Still, as his wife, I knew deep inside that something wasn't right, but I figured some righteousness is better than none. I can remember hoping and praying that when my husband returned home from the youth retreat, he would be a new man—and he was—for about a week.

The Lord tells us He wants us hot or cold. In Revelation 3:15–16, He says that he will spew lukewarm souls out of his mouth. Was my husband lukewarm or was he flat-out cold? Honestly, I became irritated that these church people were so naive to think that my husband and I were in the same boat. How was I ever to get prayer warriors to help me believe for a miracle when everyone classified us as being the "perfect couple"? I felt like one crying out in the wilderness, but no one heard my despair. Where was the accountability that my husband needed to realize his walk was counterfeit?

In the midst of all of these years that passed, I had no idea I was living out a picture of Christ before my husband that would prove to be the very "power" that would bring him to repent. Ultimately, this picture of Christ was the message of love that would save our marriage.

Humanly speaking, I loved my husband, and he loved me. We just had different views on spiritual matters and biblical truths. My views were based upon the Holy Spirit's teachings, and his were based upon his own "intellectual interpretation." While this may sound like a minor difference to some, it would prove to be the most important factor in our marriage. Jesus is the only glue that can hold a marriage together. It doesn't matter how much you love each other, life has a way of pulling people apart. If a married man and woman are not both born of the spirit, the enemy can get a foothold in that relationship.

> *The thief cometh not, but for to steal, and to kill, and to destroy: I am come that they might have life, and that they might have it more abundantly.*
> —JOHN 10:10

This is why it is so important for us to teach our children the importance of being "equally yoked." Even though God's Word commands us to not enter into marriage with an unbeliever, the scriptures also teach us about covenant relationships. This means, once you have been bonded together before the Lord (whether equally yoked or not), you must work through such difficulties. This can take many years or even a lifetime to fulfill and will be a battle fought with many tears. It is best to teach our children the importance of not dating unbelievers.

> *Be ye not unequally yoked together with unbelievers: for what fellowship hath righteousness with unrighteousness? and what communion hath light with darkness?*
> —2 Corinthians 6:14

Life Application

Marriage is a covenant. Once you are made one flesh by the supernatural power of God, you must work through difficulties that arise throughout life, no matter how painful. As you do your part—by doing what God commands of you—the Lord will do His part by arranging circumstances in your favor.

For more instruction on how to live an example of godly character before your husband, read 1 Peter 3.

three

SEEKING DESTINY

LIFE LESSONS

- You were created for a very specific and unique purpose.
- Christian women should embrace seasons of change, reserving the necessary years needed to raise their children in a warm, godly home.
- God's blessings will overflow when you are submissive to His plans for your life.

To every thing there is a season, and a
time to every purpose under heaven.

—ECCLESIASTES 3:1

L
ET ME TAKE you back to my professional life for a moment. As I had mentioned earlier, I owned and operated three dance studios for twenty years. Believe it or not, I actually opened my first dance studio at the tender age of sixteen—that's a testimony reserved for another book. While I

do not recommend opening a business at such a young age, God definitely had His hand upon me, working everything out for my good and His glory.

When I first started my business, I was a young teenager full of dreams. Not knowing God or understanding His plans and purposes for my life, I was easily distracted. There were many well-meaning supporters from my small community who encouraged me to open a dance studio while still in high school. It seemed opening this small business was just the pacifier I needed to keep me busy and quiet—until time for graduation.

Fast forward thirteen years... Still teaching dance—now with three locations—I prided myself on having a competitive edge. My notability quickly spread across the nation as one who cultivated dancers of excellence. Sporting a reputation for stepping out of the box with masterpiece choreography, my dancers oftentimes wore costumes that were a little more revealing than most. (This was in the 1980s and early 1990s. Risky things I did then are considered very normal now.)

As you can imagine, once I became born-again, I felt as though I was living a double standard. How could I worship the Lord on Sundays and then go into my dance studios during the week and teach the youth of my community using secular music that suggested lust, sexual sin, pride, divorce, gangs, partying, and so on? You see, I never heard the words to these songs when I was lost. I usually selected music primarily for the beat. Now that the Lord had opened my ears to the lyrics of the world's tunes, I was ashamed to let these songs ring out in my classroom.

I began to sense the Lord preparing me to change the musical format of my studios. Then one day, as I was arranging shoes in my home closet, the Lord startled me as I heard Him audibly speak, "DEBORAH, I WANT YOU TO BE ALL MINE." This was the confirmation I needed to begin searching—in obedience—for music that would not be offensive to my Lord. This world carelessly taints the innocent consciousness of our children today, and I no longer wanted any part of it. The days of assisting Satan to perpetuate his carnival of evil devices were over!

I had no idea where I would find enough music to support several mega dance recitals each year. It was an even bigger mystery as to how I would find Christian music suitable for tap, jazz, lyrical, and ballet. Not wanting to lose the momentum my clients were accustomed to, it took a leap of faith for me to even "think" such a transition could take place without a hitch. Going from the sounds of the world to the sounds of God's kingdom, especially in business, was pretty radical. How would I ever be able to produce the quality productions that my audience demanded once I changed to the tune of the gospel?

God is so good! Here again, He answered my prayer. That same year, He birthed a Christian radio station in our community that was like none other before. This station introduced me to the wonderful sounds of contemporary Christian artists I had never heard of, making it possible for me to officially launch my new format of dance ministry.

In all of my years of dance, I had never heard of dance ministry. I really thought, at first, I had started something new. In fact, the first couple of years my studios existed as a dance ministry, I never met anyone else doing the same thing. Little did I know the Lord had birthed these Christian dance studios all over the world. I would soon meet many others that shared in the same vision the Lord had given to me. Incredibly amazing!

My first Christian dance production was quite a jolt to an unsuspecting audience who had been accustomed to our yearly Vegas-style performances. The name of that first show was *Don't Overlook Salvation*. It was humbling to witness so many tears as on-lookers could hardly catch their breath trying to speak at the end of the night. This was the first time I had ever encountered my choreography touching people in such a powerful way. Finally, my career had meaning and purpose! I was determined to use my talents to glorify God from that point on.

I would spend the next seven years of my dance studio career creating works of inspiration that led people to the cross. Incorporating Bible studies and prayer into my rehearsals, the Lord taught me to make the most of my time spent with the vast numbers of youth who came through my establishment. Many of these dancers were a part of my program for up to fifteen years. While some had never heard about Jesus, still others were churchgoers—but never thought being a Christian could be fun. Our days of dance ministry together shook our community for Christ in a profound way. It was an awesome time in my career.

Keep in mind, during all of this time of incredible ministry, my husband was still lost, and he usually showed up at these anointed dance concerts smelling of alcohol—we were not a team. My husband was very supportive and extremely proud of my reputation in the community as a professional dance teacher, but when it came to watching these anointed presentations of the gospel, he would always watch from a distance. He usually didn't stay for the entire presentation once I switched to Christian music. Again, that was too close to the fire for someone not ready to surrender.

I can remember so many years of praying for the Lord to open the doors of destiny in my life. Even though my dance ministry appeared to be exactly what God would have me do, I sensed a larger vision peering through the corners of my soul. I did not know what this calling was, but I had a restlessness to press in and find out what "God's perfect will" was for my life. I can recall so many intimate prayer times with the Lord, crying out for Him to reveal to me the desires of my heart. It seemed my heart's desires were somehow being suppressed by my busy lifestyle. I truly believe that most people will never recognize the desires of their heart because of the mundane daily life cycles that have kept them spinning on the same treadmill year after year. I couldn't stand the thought of growing old, only to realize I had missed my purpose in life.

Up until this point in my Christian walk I had always asked God for things that seemed attainable to me. I could understand Him using me in a dance studio ministry because that is where my comfort zone was; but, to be used in any way beyond the boundaries of my professional career in the performing arts (my realm of personal and professional influence) was inconceivable to me.

As I sought the Lord, day after day, desperately wanting to find my purpose, I quickly recognized, again, that I was wavering in my prayers. One day I was asking the Lord to build my business into a multi-million dollar dance ministry that could be duplicated around the world, and the next day I was asking the Lord to give me more time at home with my children. I was torn between being a godly wife and mother, and being a godly mover and shaker for the entire world. (Earlier in this book we discovered the consequences of being double minded, according to God's Word. I couldn't expect anything from God; my prayers were being tossed about like the waves of the sea.)

So many people today are living out their lives in a routine they think to be God's plan. Most people are conditioned to wear the "mask of happiness." They play the role like an Academy Award winner, day after day, month after month, and year after year. I believe most people do not have a clue of what the desire of their heart is. They do not have a God-ordained purpose and are not living to leave a legacy from generation to generation. Don't finish your life with hidden treasures of your soul left unfound. Instead, pray that God would give you the desires of your heart, knowing that He wants to do just that!

> *Delight thyself also in the* LORD: ***and he shall give thee the desires of thine heart.***
> —PSALM 37:4, EMPHASIS ADDED

In chapter three of Ecclesiastes the Word of God says that there is a time and season for everything in life. It is so important for wives and mothers to understand their significance in the home. The devil wants us to believe that if we are not equally bringing in money for our household or if we are not creating a career outlet for ourselves, we have missed our calling. This is a crippling mirage of family wholeness. God has purposed families to be established with order, the man being the head of the household (under Christ) and the woman being his helpmate (Genesis 2:18). Women today need to acknowledge the importance of being an encourager to their husband and a nurturer to their children. Raising our children is something we only get one shot at, so we had better make every moment count while we can. There will be plenty of time later in life to take on a career, if that is God's plan. Break out of that superwoman costume! It's time to put on your robe of righteousness by carefully listening to the Holy Spirit and searching the scriptures for wisdom on how to live a virtuous life. (Proverbs 31 speaks of the virtuous woman.)

In my sincere petitions concerning God's plan for my life, He began to reveal the steps I would need to take in order to walk in my God-ordained destiny. The Lord taught me I would need to leave the ninety-nine and go after the one (Luke 15:4–7). It was God's will for me to give up my career, for a season, to focus on "living out Christ" before my family. Before the Lord made this clear to me, I was all about "works." I thought that my works for Him was what He wanted. The Lord was showing me that He wanted to work "through me"; He did not need me working "for Him." This wooing of the Holy Spirit was requiring me to lay down my life in a way that I had never imagined for the cause of Christ.

> *Then said Jesus unto his disciples, If any man will come after me, let him deny himself, and take up his cross, and follow me. For whosoever will save his life shall lose it: and whosoever will lose his life for my sake shall find it.*
>
> —MATTHEW 16:24–25

In my reasoning, I was more than a little slow at getting the full picture. It took about three years for me to come to a point of complete surrender in my career. Slowly, I chiseled down from three studios to two. A few years later I downsized again to one.

But then, the Lord asked me for *everything*!

He even wanted my one remaining studio—the only one I had! I wish I could report to you how easily I gave the last one up. No, instead, I put out a fleece with the Lord. I pleaded, "Lord, it is just too painful for me to completely give up my career. It's all I know! It's who I am! If you really want me to completely stop my dance studio business, You will have to take it from me." That is exactly what He did! Sending a precious couple who offered to buy my building and business—when it had not even been advertised as being for sale—was the supernatural "sign" I was looking for. I knew, beyond the shadow of a doubt, this was the Lord's will. Still, this process was very painful, both emotionally and spiritually. I lost my identity once there were no more platforms for my talents. My ever-wandering visionary mind and entrepreneurial spirit had come to a crashing halt!

> *Be still, and know that I am God: I will be exalted among the heathen, I will be exalted in the earth.*
> —PSALM 46:10

I knew in my spirit that the Lord was taking away the old to build up something new. Even so, I had no idea of what the "new" would be. Holding tight to His character, I trusted my heavenly Father for His best!

So many people told me that I had missed God. I even had

people who once loved me (so I thought) turn their backs on me. Others whined with comments of disgust, "You have abandoned me in my need for a Christian dance teacher." Selling my Christian Dance Studios proved to be, as I perceived it, my first painful episode of betrayal since I had become a born-again believer. I could feel the devil laughing at me and mocking me through these former employees and clients. It was obvious that many of them did not want to "let go" and "let God." I felt as though no one cared about my family and me. It was as if time stood still—as people I once knew suddenly made me invisible. The comments, cold shoulders, looks of disbelief and disappointment, and unscriptural religious advice was like a dark cloud sent to try and make me doubt what I had just done.

When the studio finally closed at the bank, I thought my husband would see my devotion to him and Christ in such a way that he would run to the cross for salvation. My thoughts were, "OK, God, I gave it all up, now pour out my miracle!" Here again, I was awakened to the reality that my breakthrough would be a lot tougher to obtain than what I had hoped. I would have to wait on God's promise for my household to be saved. In fact, things got a lot worse before they got better.

> *And not only so, but we glory in tribulations also: knowing that tribulation worketh patience; And patience, experience; and experience, hope: And hope maketh not ashamed; because the love of God is shed abroad in our hearts by the Holy Ghost which is given unto us.*
>
> —ROMANS 5:3–5

Everybody knows, oil and water don't mix—just like righteousness and ungodliness don't mix. Satan was waging war on my destiny; his strategy was to destroy my marriage, my children, my testimony, our finances, and every ounce of faith in God's Word that I had worked so hard to develop. The devil is a thief that will stop at nothing to accomplish his goal. If he can't keep you from going to heaven, he will do everything he knows to thwart your destiny, to render your life powerless for the kingdom of God. He cannot stand to see people—who are created in the image of God—figure out who they were meant to be, because he knows that God's children are more than conquerors!

LIFE APPLICATION

The devil already knows he is defeated, but he wants to make you "think" he is really giving God a headache. He wants to make you "think" God can't or won't come through in your situation. If you want to get your miracle DON'T LISTEN TO YOUR ADVERSARY!

To learn more about the heritage of the servants of the Lord, read Isaiah 54.

four

BREAKING GENERATIONAL CURSES

LIFE LESSONS

- Your marriage is worth fighting for.
- Sometimes things must get worse before they get better.
- Your testimony may be the example that draws many family members to Christ.

For as the body without the spirit is dead,
so faith without works is dead also.

—JAMES 2:26

URING MY TIME of waiting on the Lord, things were getting incredibly worse, instead of better. The Lord began to uncover my husband's "secret sins": this is the dreadful phase of my testimony I commonly refer to as "the shakedown." It never crossed my mind that I would ever suffer through a marital odyssey with so much heartbreak. Even before my wedding day, I always said, "I would never be married to an alcoholic, and I would most definitely divorce an unfaithful husband." These were words I would soon have to "eat" if I were to be victorious in the struggle for my marriage to be healed. The only person I could change was me! Only God could change my husband.

> *Create in me a clean heart, O God; and renew a right spirit within me.*
>
> —PSALM 51:10

These sins that the Lord began to uncover were what seemed to be a weekly, and sometimes daily, nightmare for me. Financial blows began to surface, one after another. Everything from the doorbell ringing, only to find some angry bill collector accusing me of things I knew nothing about, to gambling buddies dunning us for bets unpaid. When the surprising back taxes, penalties, and interest were added, our debt grew to such an enormous amount, it seemed there would be no way we could ever repay it all.

Here is how it all started to unravel...

After the final sale of my studio, my husband's business folded. Here we both were with no job and more bills due than we ever had in our lives. I had no idea my husband's company was in trouble at the time that I sold my last studio, and I am certain that had I known about the condition of his finances, my faith in following God's plan—to walk away from my career—would have been weakened. Regardless of his reason for keeping this a secret, I felt deceived. In agony I protested, "Why didn't you share your business endeavors with me?" Feeling we had no teamwork in our marriage and no vision for our future, it was as if everything I had worked for over the past twenty years was being sucked into a vacuum. Slothful decisions, I had no control over, brought an overshadowing spirit of hopelessness. It was overwhelming.

Now the pornography secrets were something that I had stumbled upon several times throughout our marriage. I was always told, "Those books are not mine, they are my brothers" and "I don't know why those images pop up on the computer screen." These findings would always leave me feeling ugly, unimportant, cheated, and violently angry. For the most part, my husband had become a master at hiding his lustful addictions, because he knew the torment it put me through. I could not bare the thought of my husband looking at these beautifully airbrushed portraits of naked women. As pretty as I had hoped to be, there was no way I could ever compare to an enhanced photograph. In this season, God exposed all sin—nothing was held back. Forced to face the fact that pornography was an ongoing part of my husband's lifestyle, I was crushed.

The golf and gambling revelations were further daggers to my heart. The Lord began to uncover the true amount of time my husband spent on the golf course. People that are lost in their sins will justify their behavior; they will even flat-out lie. Once a person lets the devil lead them down that self-serving path of destruction, they begin to dig themselves into a hole that just keeps getting deeper and deeper. While I thought my husband was diligently working, he was actually spending three and four days per week gambling on the golf course. I couldn't comprehend his reasoning for wanting to place bets— with wealthy men—when we couldn't even keep our bills paid. To think of settling a bet with someone who did not need our money made me furious!

The gambling didn't stop there. Satan has a multitude of

avenues for the addictive soul. There are some highly sophisticated "businesses" that work the odds for every sports game on television. Then, there are also those private betting rings in every hometown offering the same sinful thrill. Thank goodness, we didn't live in a state where gambling was legalized! If so, I cannot imagine where we would have ended up.

This "unveiling season" lasted for what seemed to be an eternity. I cried in prayer, "Lord, please don't show me anything else! I cannot handle another disappointment in my marriage." That's one prayer that the Lord chose not to answer. Instead, the next three years were a time of the "truth being exposed." The worst was yet to come. This was a "shakedown"!

> *Therefore judge nothing before the time, until the Lord come, who both will bring to light the hidden things of darkness, and make manifest the counsels of the hearts: and then shall every man have praise of God.*
> —1 CORINTHIANS 4:5

During the first two years of this grueling ordeal, the Lord confined me to homeschooling our children. Up until the sale of my dance studios, I had kept my children in Christian school. It started out as Christian day care and then went on to kindergarten and elementary education. When our household had two incomes, Christian school was a bill I didn't mind paying. I had made a commitment to the Lord when our children were in my womb that I would raise them up to know Him. I was determined to make sure my children's minds were not influenced by secular humanism. For me, this vow could only be fulfilled by the promise of a godly education.

Needless to say, once my business no longer existed, private school was not possible. The school's principle suggested that I consider homeschooling and, initially, this idea was offensive and completely out of the question. After all, I was a dance teacher; I knew nothing about elementary education. In my failed attempts to try and figure out a way to keep my children in their Christian school, I fell in desperation at the feet of Jesus. I sobbed, "Lord, tell me what to do!" What was God's will in my dilemma? Was it for me to put my children in public school, or was He going to supernaturally make a way for my children to attend their Christian school? Surely, the Lord wouldn't ask me to home school. I begged the Lord to make a way for us to continue at our Christian school, but here again, this was not the Lord's plan during this season of my life.

I can remember the Lord specifically showing me in His Word what needed to be done in order to stop these generational curses that were manifesting in my husband's life from coming upon our children. The Lord was teaching me how to come against iniquity in their bloodline. In order to follow through with the Lord's instruction, I would need to "beef up" on my life application skills as a mom. This would involve me teaching my children right from wrong—according to God's Word—and it would involve me speaking truth into their young lives at every opportunity. I was about to become a mercy and truth teacher in such a way that demons would have to flee. The blood of Jesus was about to be applied, not only spiritually but also physically, as my blood—my life—would be poured out by the sacrificial giving of myself. I would spend the next two years standing in the gap, as a home-school mom, for the sake of my children's souls.

*By mercy and truth iniquity is purged: and by the fear of
the* LORD *men depart from evil.*

—PROVERBS 16:6

To help you better understand iniquity; consider someone
having a bend toward sin in their personality. We hear so much
about DNA today as being the reason for certain behavior traits
that are passed from one generation to another. The iniquity of
a person is like the spiritual DNA that causes that person to
habitually sin. In my husband's family, alcoholism is an addictive demon that has sought to destroy the lives of generation
after generation. This repetitive cycle in his family tree would
be an outward manifestation of the "generational curse" in his
bloodline.

My family history was also threatened with iniquities, desiring to creep in to paralyze, defeat, and destroy my
children and me. Glory to God! Now that I had become a born-
again child of the King, my iniquities had been purged by the
precious blood of Jesus. I was set free from the bondage of sin
and death the day I made Christ my Lord and Savior.

*But he was wounded for our transgressions, he was bruised
for our iniquities: the chastisement of our peace was upon
him; and with his stripes we are healed.*

—ISAIAH 53:5

God will often choose one family member to accomplish
the work of salvation in the lives of every generation both
forward and backward. In other words, the Lord will use one
obedient soul to influence and pray for, not only their own
husband, children, and grandchildren; but, He will also use
that person to bring about salvation in their parents, siblings,

and grandparents. As in the life of Abraham, God is calling someone who will obey His voice and forsake family traditions, to live out a testimony that perpetuates salvation in that entire family tree! God will break the curses that have been passed down through the years if someone will stand bold to fight the good fight of faith, not giving into the lies of the enemy. Breaking the curse will require faith in God's Word and it will require sacrifice.

> *Greater love hath no man than this, that a man lay down his life for his friends.*
>
> —JOHN 15:13

In my determination to win the battle that was seeking to destroy our family, God humbled me to the realization that homeschooling was, indeed, His plan for me in this upcoming season of our lives. My feelings of inadequacy were somewhat calmed once I fully reckoned them (my children) as only rising to kindergarten and second grade in this first year of our homeschooling experience. Plus, some friends of mine who also felt called to home school were of great encouragement as we started our venture together. Thankfully, God only required me to home school for two years, but I can honestly tell you that it was the most important two years of my children's education. So many times my children would ask me tough questions about their dad's behavior or other things they didn't understand about their grandparents' second marriages. I am so glad I was there "at that moment" to give them godly explanations of truth!

> *And ye shall know the truth, and the truth shall make you free.*
>
> —JOHN 8:32

Although my professional career had ended (at least for an undetermined season), my new life as a stay-at-home wife and mother had just begun. The Lord had pruned and rearranged my life in such a way that "I" was no longer in charge. Each day proved to be a new adventure as I was learning to be totally dependent upon God's every Word for daily direction. I must admit I felt awkward, sometimes bored, insignificant, and completely out of place throughout many of my homeschooling days. Even so, it was a time I do not regret. The Lord was redeeming the time I had spent away from my children. All the years of guilt that I carried each time I left my babies in the care of strangers—while I chased after my career—were about to be restored. Perfect peace.

LIFE APPLICATION

Breaking generational curses will require faith in God's Word. and it will require sacrifice.

Is God asking you to lay your life down so someone else can live?

To better understand the meaning of this question, read John 15.

five

FOLLOWING THE HOLY SPIRIT

LIFE LESSONS

- Guidance—Victorious Christian living requires that believers cultivate their ability to "hear" and "obey" the voice of the Holy Spirit.
- Power—Victorious Christians are not afraid to be fully equipped and confident in storming the powers of darkness.
- Peace—Victorious Christian living is realized as believers seek to follow after peace in their decision-making.
- Submission—Victorious Christian wives understand the significance of submitting to their husband.

God is a Spirit: and they that worship him must worship him in spirit and in truth.

—JOHN 4:24

L ET'S TAKE A break from my story for a moment. In doing so, I'd like to share some spiritual truths the Lord opened my understanding to during those twelve long years that were spent praying for my miracle. By now, I hope you have a vivid picture of my married life, identifying with the debilitating warfare our family endured. Prayerfully, my transparency will bring to light some similarities in your own life that you must deal with, in order for God to make your family whole. This book is intended to inspire you and to help you remain strong and of good courage, until your breakthrough comes (Joshua 1:6). God is no respecter of persons. What He did for me, He'll do for you—keep believing!

TRUTH NO. 1: THE INDWELLING HOLY SPIRIT

*Behold, **to obey is better than sacrifice**, and to harken than the fat of rams.*
—1 SAMUEL 15:22, EMPHASIS ADDED

Let's look at the importance of following the Holy Spirit in every decision you make, both big and small.

The Holy Spirit comes to dwell in every born-again believer at his or her moment of conversion. This is the actual Spirit of God Himself living on the inside of His children. The precious Holy Spirit shows us all truth and guides us in every area of our lives, as we observe to submit our will to His. The true test of our character lies in our obedience (or disobedience) upon hearing the voice of the Holy Spirit. God gives us a choice. We can either follow His ways, which lead to life; or, He will allow us to forge ahead with our own plans, oftentimes resulting in bondage and hardship.

So often, I'll hear Christians say, "How do I know if I'm hearing the voice of the Holy Spirit or if I'm just thinking things up in my mind?" Learning to hear and recognize the voice of the Holy Spirit is a walk of faith that must be tried and tested in every Christian's life. I think every born-again believer has questioned the voices in their head—at one time or another. Actually, until a Christian has grown in his or her understanding of Scripture enough to know the character God, it is always a good idea to look for confirmation before making radical decisions based upon a thought. The more mature we become in Christ, the easier it will be to discern the voice of God from others.

> *My sheep hear my voice, and I know them, and they follow me.*
>
> —JOHN 10:27

In explaining how someone can distinguish the voice of God from the voice of the devil (Satan will masquerade as an angel of light), consider the following analogies:

- The voice of the Holy Spirit can be compared to that of your conscious.

- The Holy Spirit always speaks in accordance with the Word of God.

- The Holy Spirit is a gentleman. His words are pleasant and not over-bearing or oppressive.

- The voice of God often comes as an overriding thought or "quickening" that gets your attention.

- Some names for the Holy Spirit that describe His character are: Comforter, Teacher, Counselor, Wisdom, Knowledge, Understanding, Power, Life, Truth, Holiness, Grace, Fear of the Lord, Joy, Judgment, Glory.

It is imperative that Christians develop a relationship with the Holy Spirit, learning to hear, know, and obey His voice. In fact, some things the Spirit of God warns us about can be detrimental, if not promptly heeded. Keeping a marriage together and a family intact, over the course of a lifetime, will require one to follow the leading of the Holy Spirit.

TRUTH NO. 2: FOLLOW PEACE

*Flee also youthful lusts: but **follow** righteousness, faith, charity, **peace**, with them that call on the Lord out of pure heart.*
—2 TIMOTHY 2:22, EMPHASIS ADDED

Learning to follow after peace, according to God's Word, will always bring great rewards. Let me warn you, following peace does not always mean following logic. In fact, I have found God will often allow two or more choices to be placed in front of me—each seemingly good—whenever I am at a crossroads of decision in my life. Many times, the choice that doesn't make logical sense is the one that will, ultimately, bring peace to my soul. "Spiritual truths" and "worldly truths" are not always interchangeable.

The Scripture says, "What is a man profited, if he shall gain the whole world and lose his own soul?" (Matthew 16:26). Your soul is your mind, your will, and your emotions. In meditating on this passage of Scripture, I came to realize I was sacrificing my soul in exchange for my career. My lust for the things of this world (money, stuff, man's approval) was overpowering my desire to be a godly wife and mother. Once the Lord peeled away the superficial layers of my character—by allowing me to hang out in the valley of decision—my spirit began to rule over my flesh, as I longed for the simpler things in life. Pruning is not a fond aspect of growing in Christ, but once the process is complete, our lives look more like His.

I'm not saying it is God's will for every woman to quit her job once she has children. What I am saying is, "God has a specific path that leads to peace for each one of His children." The key to making tough decisions, even when several choices seem right, is to follow the road that leads to peace. I have found the Lord will always supply my needs as I seek to obey Him with a peaceful heart and mind.

Decide now to make choices that give your soul peace!

TRUTH NO. 3: YOU RECEIVE POWER, WHEN THE HOLY GHOST COMES UPON YOU!

*Follow after charity, **and desire spiritual gifts**, but rather that ye may prophecy.*
—1 CORINTHIANS 13:8, EMPHASIS ADDED

Many of you reading this book may not have knowledge of the "gifts of the Spirit." Maybe your church doesn't teach about spiritual gifts, either because these gifts don't fit into their doctrine of beliefs, or perhaps, because of a lack of understanding. Whatever the reason, I'd like to challenge some of you in your thinking, just for a moment, regarding the "power" that is available to all of God's children.

The way I see it, God didn't put passages of Scripture about spiritual gifts into the Bible for the purpose of creating confusion. The devil is the only author of confusion that I know. God's enemy has worked overtime throughout the ages to scramble man's opinion on spiritual gifts because he knows *this is where the power is.* If you want to plug into the "power of God," you will need to crucify any misunderstandings, fears, or negative teachings residing in your soul. Think about it: supernatural manifestations within the kingdom of God are natural occurrences from a spiritual God.

During my twelve years of believing God for a born-again husband, I don't know how I would have persevered without some of the encouraging prophecies spoken over me, the warfare prayers, my prayer language (for those times I couldn't pray), words of knowledge, words of wisdom, prophetic dreams, and the gifts of healing.

One astonishing fact about our story is how our family lived all those years, raising our children without medical insurance, coupled with a shortage of finances. When we needed healing—we prayed! I am sure many of you reading this book are in similar situations. Your back is against the wall, and you just don't know what to do. Honey, a "double dose of the Holy Ghost" will open your eyes to a whole new world—the spiritual world of power!

Once Jesus was crucified, buried, and resurrected, He was seen by many people before His ascension to heaven. He told these "believers" they would receive power after the Holy Ghost came upon them (Acts 1:8). We also learn in the book of Acts that each time the Holy Spirit fell, there was evidence. This evidence was referred to as "praying in unknown tongues" many times throughout the book of Acts.

Since this is not a book on how to pray in an unknown tongue, I will just say a few more things to fan the flames of your curiosity about this awesome invitation the Lord gives to all believers. If you want to take a deeper plunge into the supernatural power of God, you must search the scriptures, close your ears to the naysayer, glean from others who have this gift, then seek God for your baptism! As long as you think you don't need it, you'll never get it. Begin to study Christians (of good character) who operate in spiritual gifts. Ask God to open your understanding to the importance of such gifts for the church today. (Caution: The "fruit" of a believer is always more important than the supernatural power operating in his or her life. Don't be discouraged by immature Christians or impostors.)

Jesus Christ the same yesterday, and today, and forever.
—Hebrews 13:8

Remember, hell has waged war against you and your family. The battle you are fighting is a demonic attack that cannot be fought in your own strength. Many Christians have lost the battle over breaking generational curses, because they have tried to fight supernatural principalities and powers with human weapons. You are not wrestling against flesh and blood, but against rulers of the darkness and spiritual wickedness in high places (Ephesians 6:12). Don't be afraid of God's spiritual gifts. The devil is not going to hold back just because you don't want to engage him in battle. Gear up, and conquer in the name of Jesus!

Let's go back to my story...

In my journey to breakthrough, the Lord taught me precept-upon-precept, in His Word, how to press through and overcome defeat. At each crisis I faced, the leading of the Holy Spirit (and my obedience or my disobedience following that leading) determined the outcome. Each trial was yet another layer of the onion to my soul that had to be pealed away, in order for deliverance to take place. God wants us to be whole! He is not interested in putting Band-Aids on our lives so that we can have temporary comfort. Instead, He wants to make us whole from the inside—out! Don't be discouraged during these trying times. God is at work, even when you don't feel His presence.

I came to realize that each victory and each setback was just another part of the process that was needed, in order to bring about wholeness to our family. To be honest, I just wanted the Lord to "zap" my husband and cause him to be a born-again man of God—*immediately*! I wasn't interested in the process during the agonizing time that I spent going through it; but now that I am on the other side looking back, I can honestly say, "I am glad for the Lord's pruning of both my husband and me." I truly got more than I asked, or even thought to pray for, once my breakthrough finally came. The heavenly reality of being married to a born-again man of God is so much more romantic, intimate, and exciting than I ever imagined! God is so good and He truly gives good gifts to His children (Matthew 7:11).

I am proclaiming, "Hold onto the horns of the altar and cry

out for your miracle, your breakthrough!" Don't give up just because you don't see any change right away. In fact, things may sometimes get worse before they get better.

Truth No. 4: Submit to Your Own Husband

*Wives, submit yourselves unto your **own** husbands, as unto the Lord.*
—Ephesians 5:22, emphasis added

God revealed a *rhema* word to me from 1 Peter 3 during my many years of praying, waiting, and believing in Him for a miracle. In this passage of Scripture, wives are instructed to be in subjection to, and to love, their "own husbands." As I pondered why the word *own* was used in this and many other scriptures pertaining to a wife submitting to her husband, the Lord showed me that I was praying incorrectly. He rebuked me for wanting my husband to be like the preacher, or like other godly men that I knew. The Lord told me to love my husband just as he was, to honor and respect him—just like he was. This came as a shock to me! At that time in our marriage, my husband was not making good decisions. He was "lost", self-centered, and always seeking to drink beer and "live it up." This wasn't the kind of man I expected God to tell me to respect. After all, my husband rarely wanted to do anything godly.

The Lord taught me that He would be with me, no matter where I went and no matter what consequences resulted from the bad choices made by my spouse.

Surrendering what I knew to be right in order for my husband to experience failures was not in my nature. I have a "classic type-A" personality, always wanting things perfect and in order. Nevertheless, in allowing the Lord to work in the life of my spouse, God required me to give up the reigns. He also pointed out to me that I was coveting other women's husbands by wanting mine to be righteous "like theirs." It wasn't that God didn't want my husband righteous, but He didn't want my husband to be like theirs. God wanted my husband to be all of who He created "him" to be. Are you limiting God by wanting what someone else has?

What a picture of Christ I was learning to live out in front of my husband's eyes. He was witnessing a metamorphosis of my behavior, as I allowed him the freedom of making choices for himself. God did not call me to be my husband's mother. I was to be his wife. It would take a lot of prayer for me to submit to my husband while he was still a sinner, but with the Lord's help, I somehow surrendered my will to His. Don't misunderstand my position, I was not "silent" in what I knew to be right, but I did not insist on getting my way either (1 Corinthians 13:4-8).

In my earliest years of salvation, I would not be caught dead with a glass of wine. Still today, I do not drink alcohol and have no intentions of drinking any. I believe I am called to ministry, and there is no room for drinking in my calling. I also think it is important for Christians to be a living testimony, not causing others to stumble. My husband is a former alcoholic, and I would never want to be a stumbling block in his life.

On the other hand, drinking wine does not necessarily mean you are a sinner. Once you are born again, you are given the freedom to eat and drink anything that does not go against your conscience, providing you are not a glutton or a drunkard. Some of you may find this next story to be surprising at first, but I hope the Lord will help you see it is important to "listen" closely to the work of the Holy Spirit in every situation you encounter, along your journey. Religion is not what brings others to the cross of Jesus (Romans 14:17). Love is the most powerful force. *Love never fails* (1 Corinthians 13)!

At various moments throughout my twelve-year span, the Holy Spirit oftentimes led me to not be so "stiff" around my husband. In recalling a very romantic vacation the two of us shared, I remember my husband wanting me to join him with a glass of wine, and I did. I did not want or need the wine, but through my husband's eyes, I was not making myself so holy that I was untouchable. I could sense the presence of the Holy Spirit throughout that entire vacation. I am sure that the Lord revealed Himself to my husband through my sincere desire to be a loving wife instead of a religious nag. I did not make drinking wine a habit, nor did I begin to act as though his excessive drinking was acceptable. I just tried to keep our marriage in balance by not making myself appear to be so holy that my husband felt intimidated.

Well, I know that last paragraph may have just blown some of your super-religious minds, but I felt like I needed to include that part of my story in this book. One of you may be facing the same difficulty. It's like this, the Bible tells us it is wrong to kill, but we also read in Ecclesiastes, there is a time to kill. I know if I were drafted to serve in the U.S. military to fight in combat, my Lord would tell me how to fight the enemy. I have all confidence this same Holy Spirit that brings life would speak to me about killing, if my life were in danger. I'm not saying killing is good, but I hope this illustration will help you to see that our Savior is "Lord" over all situations. If you want to win the battle that is threatening to destroy your home, you must take orders from the Holy Spirit, trusting in the Lord's ability to show Himself strong on your behalf.

Another example of which I followed the leading of the Holy Spirit when it didn't seem logical was when my husband insisted on taking me to a comedy show that was not the kind of place where a Christian should be seen. I did not want to go, and I told my husband that I didn't want to go. After he begged, pouted, and pleaded, I decided to pray for help in knowing what to do. I was stunned! The Lord told me to go; He would be with me. Would you believe, the first comedian on the stage that night actually witnessed for Jesus? Surely he was a new convert continuing to work in this secular line of comedy shows (most of which are vulgar with foul language). You could have heard a pin drop during his act, and I am sure I was the only one laughing at his jokes! I was laughing and praising God for His faithfulness, while my husband was astonished—actually spooked. He "knew" at that moment that the God I served was real, and he knew that my Lord was looking after me. I think my husband could actually feel the breath of God on his back. Hallelujah!

There are so many other times the Lord met me in awkward places and strange situations. He is so faithful! The Lord would always do the work, if I would just "surrender." Now this does not mean I gave up or gave in. Never! I was just trying to listen to the guidance of the Holy Spirit. I was trying to be obedient, sometimes just to make it through the moment, sometimes expecting my miracle at that moment.

Behold, I send an Angel before thee, to keep thee in the way, and to bring thee into the place which I have prepared. Beware of him, and obey his voice, provoke him not; for he will not pardon your transgressions: for my name is in him. But if thou shalt indeed obey his voice, and do all that I speak; then I will be an enemy unto thine enemies, and an adversary unto thine adversaries.

—EXODUS 23:20–22

LIFE APPLICATION

There is a remnant of believers that will trust God against all odds. This remnant will seek to do His will. Will you pledge to be an elite follower of Jesus by *doing* the will of the Father? Read the second chapter of James to study how faith should work in the life of the believer.

Early career days, 1980s

Praise Dance in the late 1990s

1984 wedding portrait

Wedding day! August 25, 1984

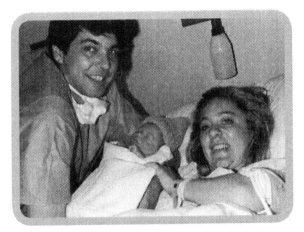

Precious memories: as love grows so does the family.
This is the birth of Preston—just minutes old.

On vacation in Myrtle Beach, SC

Birthdays are always fun; Garrett and Preston

There is nothing like family time—birthday fun.

The boys loved to dress in superhero costumes.
Garrett is Batman and Preston is Superman.

My fortieth birthday

Swimming with stingrays

Hang gliding with my sons

Our home for over 15 years—the one God allowed us to keep!

July 2008, Preston's 16th birthday

Preston, me, Jay, and Garrett (in the front)—
our family's Disney vacation

Brazil 2007 mission trip

This is the first day that Jay ever preached a message
after becoming a born-again child of God!

November 2009

six

VISION OR PERISH?

LIFE LESSONS

- Success and happiness cannot be achieved apart from God.
- Being a helpmate doesn't end when times get tough.
- God's provision is made available through tithing.

This book of the law shall not depart out of thy mouth; but thou shalt meditate therein day and night, that thou mayest observe to do according to all that is written therein: for then thou shalt make thy way prosperous, and then thou shalt have good success.

—JOSHUA 1:8

RELENTLESSLY TRYING TO find success (apart from God), my husband began to search for a job. Before our career predicament, neither he nor I knew anything about working for someone else. Each of us was self-employed from high school and never imagined we'd ever be thrust into corporate America, especially upon approaching forty. Without college degrees, it seemed the world was against us as we desperately sought to get our foot in the door—just for an interview. Job-hunting at nearly forty was a rude awakening for both of us.

I prayed and encouraged, and prayed and cheered. I was determined to stay positive—full of faith—through each dead-end experience of job blunders. Thankfully, my husband's charming personality and impressive entrepreneurial background opened several doors for "commission only" sales jobs. As a master in the art-of-sales, he was confident, rising quickly to become the number-one salesperson in each company. Holding my breath, it always seemed that just before each payday would arrive, his client(s) would have trouble with financing and everything would fall through. There was always some disappointment at the end of our rainbow. We ended up with a lot of trophies (literally)—but no money to pay our bills! And so, in an effort to find income-producing employment, he wandered from one job to another; on several occasions he had more than one job at a time.

My husband became very depressed and periodically told me that he felt like a failure. I can vividly remember those sacred moments, anointing him with Wesson Oil, and praying over him before he walked out the door to face the giants. I *trusted* God, and he was glad I did. Never refusing my prayer ceremonies, he was a broken man who was hoping for the benefits of being a child of God—through association. Still, he just couldn't see that all God wanted was his heart—all of it. During our season of shakedown, there were no shortcuts to receiving the Lord's favor. It reminds me of a childhood game where you hold someone's thumb bent to the wrist, adding pressure until they say, "Uncle!" God wanted him to say, "OK, I give!"

Things got so bad that year—I can remember riding down the road, shocked to see my husband on the roof of an enormous building, working in construction. He knew nothing about this type of work and was risking his life that day to provide for his family. On top of that, the wages he earned from this particular job weren't enough to cover our groceries—much less the mortgages, utilities, and our many other household bills. I remember calling him and pleading, "Get down and come home! It's not worth it! This is not what the Lord has for you!" We didn't even have any health or hospital insurance. What would I have done if he had fallen, leaving the boys and me with medical bills heaped on top of the mounds of financial debt we were already faced with? And if he had died from such an accident, God forbid, I would then need to overcome having no husband, no career, no life insurance policy, two elementary aged children, and no income. I think my broken heart would have burst from the pressure of losing him and facing our enormous debt, coupled with no means of digging out of the hole.

I kept asking, "Honey, what do you see yourself doing?" Telling him I would support him in anything his heart desired to do, I knew that money would follow the passion. Unfortunately, many times when a man who is not following the Lord gets between a rock and a hard place, he sinks into a paralyzed state of fear. My husband was not taught (as a child) to have a vision and consequently, once the job he was familiar with was removed, he had no idea of what to do next. My husband needed a vision and fast! We were perishing as a family!

Where there is no vision, the people perish: but he that keepeth the law, happy is he.

—PROVERBS 29:18

Have you ever heard the saying; "Behind every good man, there is a good woman?" Proverbs 31:11 says the heart of a husband should safely trust in his wife. I began to seek the Lord for wisdom about how I could inspire my husband to have a vision. In fact, I plainly asked God to show me—since my husband wasn't listening—what career he should pursue to bring about financial stability for our family. I sensed the Lord saying, "Real estate!" (This was something we had never thought of before.) With lots of encouragement from me and some supernatural encounters from others in the real estate business (prayer works), my husband decided to start school. As you know, school does not pay a salary; this meant, in order for us to follow our dream, we would have to trust God to protect us financially. One thing is for sure, the Lord never suffered us to hit rock bottom. We did, however, get very close!

Finally, when real estate school was complete and licenses were in place, I just knew it would only be a matter of time before the Lord bailed us out of our grave of debt. Well, the Lord was very faithful. He sent a "big spender" to my husband for his first closing. I think we made $25,000 on that one deal. It was a miracle! Truly by the grace of God, my husband acquired this success. Ever so hopeful, I was sure this financial break-through would bring my husband to the foot of the cross... wrong again! Instead, a false assumption of the real estate business being the way to wealth came over him, and God was only a small part of the equation. (Keep in mind that $25,000 is not as much as it sounds when you owe over $500,000 and the meter is constantly running. All of our debtors wanted their money "yesterday," so most of this check was spent before it ever even hit the bank.)

Consequently (there are always consequences for disobedience), once that initial breakthrough came and went, we were plunged right back into that oppressive state of "always having more bills than we had income." My husband was having a measure of success in real estate, but this measure seemed to be just short of bailing us out. We were on a treadmill of stress, as the ups and downs of our finances never ceased to calm. It was financial torment!

> *The LORD shall open unto thee his good treasure, the heaven to give the rain unto thy land in his season, and to bless all the work of thine hand: and thou shalt lend to many nations, and thou shalt not borrow.*
> —DEUTERONOMY 28:12

> *Bring ye all the tithes into the storehouse, that there may be meat in mine house, and prove me now herewith, saith the LORD of hosts, if I will not open the windows of heaven, and pour you out a blessing, that there shall not be room enough to receive it.*
> —MALACHI 3:10

The Word of God teaches us we are to be the head and not the tail, the first and not the last, the lender and not the borrower (Deuteronomy 28:13). I knew we needed to be tithers and givers in order to open the windows of heaven and to keep the blessings of God flowing in our lives. My husband was not against tithing because he knew "the God I served" was able to give us the financial miracle we so desperately needed. So we did tithe (haphazardly), and we also gave to many in need. We gave even out of our own lack. Without a doubt, this is what kept us from utter destruction. The Lord is faithful to His Word; plus, it would have been an oxymoron for us to be the talk of the town as "financial losers" when we were observed to be giving people. I found "many" promises in God's Word that said He would keep us from being ashamed, and I stood on them. Here are a few:

> **They shall not be ashamed** in the evil time: and in the days of famine they shall be satisfied.
> —PSALM 37:19, EMPHASIS ADDED

> Uphold me according unto thy word, that I may live: and **let me not be ashamed** of my hope.
> —PSALM 119:116, EMPHASIS ADDED

Just out of reach, the blessings of God we were experiencing did not match up to the fullness of His promises that I was reading about in my Bible. We did not have financial peace. We were not able to give to others lavishly. We were always the borrower, never the lender. My mind was flooded with questions, "What is going wrong with my faith? Why doesn't the Lord completely deliver us from this mess? Will we ever experience the promises of financial blessing I've read about in God's Word?"

> The blessing of the LORD, it maketh rich and he addeth no sorrow with it.
> —PROVERBS 10:22

So I kept praying and believing that our breakthrough was just around the corner. You'd better believe, many people—both

Christians and non-Christians, alike—tried to convince me that "God may not want to bless us financially." It would drive me crazy when someone who had all of their financial needs met—with excess—would tell me that my Lord did not want our family to live in financial peace. To me, it was a slap in the face! As Christians, we should never cause the hopeful to be hopeless. We should never cause those desperate for God's deliverance to doubt their miracle will ever come. Circumstances don't negate God's will; His Word determines His will. No matter how bleak things may appear, the Bible does not lie! The Bible is God's Word, and God does not lie!

In general, I think Americans have trouble loving others enough to wholeheartedly wish financial blessings upon them. Perhaps, deep inside of many well-meaning people, there is a selfish thread that keeps them from genuinely wanting others to prosper. This is a very sad, but true, condition that needs to be purged from the hearts of all who call themselves Christians. With lip service, many will say they want you to prosper, but deep inside, their true desire is that you don't achieve any more success than they themselves have been able attain. Oftentimes, I think these selfish hearts disguise themselves with religious jargon that sounds very convincing, but is entirely unscriptural. When it comes to believing God for a financial miracle, you may find yourself being all alone as you stand on God's Word.

> *Beloved, I wish above all things that thou mayest prosper and be in health, even as thy soul prospereth.*
> —3 JOHN 1:2

Our family home, the one we had purchased many years prior, and when I had a career, was "too nice" for most people to believe that God would want us to keep it. We had nice clothes and nice cars, all of which were purchased before "God's shakedown." Unfortunately, many people could not love us enough to pray that we would not lose our home. (This reminds me of Job's friends.) Oh, how we tried for many years to sell our home. We even wanted to sell our cars. Downsizing and starting over sounded real good. But, the Lord would not give us an easy way out of this financial nightmare. He allowed us to be "trapped" for a season so He could show Himself strong on our behalf. Judgmental looks and religious catchphrases from those who didn't understand the full scope of our situation pierced my weary soul.

I remember being ashamed to wear my clothes, ashamed to drive my car, and ashamed for people to know where I lived. I knew their thoughts; they either doubted we were suffering or assumed we deserved it. The question I kept asking myself was, "Would anyone have prayed we wouldn't lose our home if we lived in a trailer instead?" My countenance fell as I shrank into myself, avoiding all forms of social activity. Others couldn't see the mighty work the Lord was doing in my husband and in me! The Lord was working on making my husband the head of our household under His authority. Jesus wanted to be Lord of our family in every heart and every mind of our home—not just mine!

> *If my people, which are called by my name, shall humble themselves, and pray, and seek my face, and turn from their wicked ways; then will I hear from heaven, and will forgive their sin, and heal their land.*
> —2 CHRONICLES 7:14

These troublesome years of living in financial captivity brought me to a new season of life. In year three, after the sale of my studios, the Lord allowed me to go back to work part-time. After two near misses in foreclosure court, I was determined to get out of this emotional hell. My husband was not responding to God's wooing.

Also, during this chapter of our life (as man and wife) the Lord revealed to me that I was hindering His process by toting my husband in my spiritual "little red wagon." The Lord wanted me to come out of the spiritual leadership role, leaving my husband to face truth alone. This is where my story begins to take a sharp turn for the worst. Just as I had always feared, my husband began to self-destruct, once my constant watch over his life was removed.

Would you believe, at the peak of my emotional and financial rollercoaster, I encountered an unexpected pregnancy? I had always wanted to have another baby, but now, at the age of thirty-nine, and with no financial security, no insurance, no home stability, and the constant shadow of depression looming over my mind, I was a little shaken—to say the least. I had no choice but go to Social Services to try and get financial aid. Hoping they would at least give me temporary insurance coverage during the nine-month pregnancy and delivery of our baby, it was a very humbling—no, it was a downright humiliating experience! We were in a tight spot. Our income was too high for governmental assistance, yet we were being crushed by our debts. I couldn't see any way—in the natural—we would ever qualify for coverage. Once again, my God made a way when there was no way!

And now for a little space grace hath been shewed from the LORD our God, to leave us a remnant to escape, and to give us a nail in his holy place, that our God may lighten our eyes, and give us a little reviving in our bondage.

—EZRA 9:8

Once the Social Services insurance coverage finally went through (about three months into the pregnancy), I made an appointment to see my doctor. I'll never forget that visit. The doctor decided to do an ultrasound to check on my progress, and as he was probing around, I noticed as his face dropped, showing deep concern. He could not find my baby's heart beat. After what seemed to be an hour—with me, the doctor, the nurse, and my sister, all frantically looking for some type of life—I was remorsefully informed that my baby was not forming properly. There was no sign of life. My doctor advised me to get a D & C, assuming I would miscarry in a few days anyway.

I was stunned! This couldn't be happening to me! It didn't make sense for the Lord to not allow the fruit of my womb to prosper. After all, His Word clearly speaks of this promise in Deuteronomy 28. I rebuked the words of that doctor and left his office confused, scared, and further vexed in my soul. Refusing to schedule the D & C, just because of a bad report from an exam, I decided to give my baby an opportunity to miraculously live. I knew I served a God of miracles. Nothing was impossible with Him.

Thou shalt not bow down to their gods...there shall nothing cast their young, nor be barren, in thy land...
—EXODUS 23:24–26

Nothing is impossible with God; however, the sovereignty of His character keeps Him from performing miracles, in certain situations, when His purposes are greater than what we can see. Spiritually speaking, there was a lot more going on behind the scenes of our family than I knew about. A terrible sin was brewing in secret—one God abhors—and consequently our pregnancy didn't have a covenant right to receive God's miracle intervention.

> *Then when lust hath conceived, it bringeth forth sin: and sin, when it is finished, bringeth forth death.*
> —JAMES 1:15

Anyway, my body did go into spontaneous miscarriage, just as the doctor predicted. I was rushed to the hospital and put to sleep by strangers (doctors and nurses) who officially performed a D & C. I was numb...

Recalling the IV, as the anesthesiologist administered my "knock-out" drug, and feeling as if my Lord had forsaken me, I really didn't care, at that moment, if I ever woke up. Yet somehow, piercing through the void of my anguish, I sensed the Lord's presence. It was as if the world stood still and the only thing alive was Him. And then...I was gone.

While I was under (in a deep sleep), and as they were performing this procedure, I had a vision. I was in God's presence, worshiping with a heavenly host of beautiful dancers. In rhythmic, slow motion praise before God's throne, our team radiantly performed a routine choreographed in splendid grandeur. This vision was so real I could even remember the ending pose when I awoke. I could feel the glory of the Lord illuminating my face as I opened my eyes and awakened from the anesthesia. I remember gazing at the nurse's shirt pocket, on which sat an angel pin of gold. I was smiling. My countenance was refreshed. That nurse probably didn't know what to think. It was as if she were a part of my vision, as I stepped from the heavenlies back into this world. It is so amazing to me how the Lord can make something beautiful out of something so ugly. He actually gave me a memory I'll never forget; a memory of His glory and splendor, in exchange for this dark moment of my life.

For I reckon that the sufferings of this present time are not worthy to be compared with the glory which shall be revealed in us.
                                            —ROMANS 8:16–18

This miscarriage incident initiated the final battle I had to conquer in order to win my husband to Christ—once and for all. Upon my recovery, and by the Lord's leading, I went back to work and gave up the reigns as "spiritual advisor" over my husband's soul. After eleven exhausting years of teaching him about the Lord, standing in the gap for him, guiding him, instructing him, making sure he went to church on Sunday mornings and so on, he was officially "on his own" with God. My role at this point was to put my efforts into restoring some financial order in our household. I set out to try and salvage what was left of our credit.

In the spirit realm, I saw our home as being built of wood planks, each breaking loose and peeling away faster than I could stand them back up. This was a horrifying vision. Like a slow death, it appeared my "happily-ever-after" marriage was slipping through my fingers. I couldn't pinpoint what was going so wrong, but I could feel the forces of darkness as they invaded my home, making it feel cold and vacant.

About a year before this eerie final phase of shakedown, the Lord allowed me to go to a different church. I left our Baptist church and began attending a very large Church of God on the edge of Charlotte. I was broken, weak, desperate, and alone. This new church offered me a place of refuge, as I sat in obscurity, hoping to glean from the charisma of these spirit-filled Christians. There was freedom of worship, strong words of encouragement, freedom to pray in tongues, and spiritually deep teachings—all of which I was so hungry for. I guess you could say I left my husband playing "Mister Counterfeit Christian" at our old church. I never fathomed he would join me, after all; he always tried to stay clear of those radical charismatic Christians. Much to my surprise, after a couple of months, he did begin to attend this church with me. He grew to love the pastor and would brag about this church to everyone. Within a year, we were members.

His excitement over the extraordinary energy of this ministry, coupled with his enjoyment of the soulful sounds of their anointed choir, still failed to break the religious spirit my husband held onto so tightly. This preacher was very blunt and to the point, preaching the Word of God and the message of salvation. Yet, my husband refused to see himself as a sinner in need of a Savior. I couldn't understand how anyone could leave that church each Sunday morning the same way they arrived. My husband just would not surrender his entire life to Jesus. "What was it going to take for him to become a born-again man of God? Would our family ever be made whole?" Unfortunately, I would be drug down one more haunted road of hell before he came to the end of himself.

After the miscarriage, I had no choice but to place my children in public school. This was completely against my will, but was necessary for a season. I was off to try my hand at corporate America. Up until this point, the Lord had only allowed me to work part-time jobs, after the sale of my business. This dark season of life I was stepping into had to happen. Oh, how I wish there could have been another way; how God wanted there to be another way. Ample opportunity had been given for my husband to repent, and now, even God turned my husband loose to self-destruct.

> *Wherefore God also gave them up to uncleanness through the lusts of their own hearts, to dishonour their own bodies between themselves.*
>
> —ROMANS 1:24

LIFE APPLICATION

Every born-again child of the King believes in God; however, not all Christians believe God wants to bless them. To further study attributes of faith, read Hebrews 11. In particular, meditate on Hebrews 11:6.

Another passage to study is Deuteronomy 28.

seven

THE MIDNIGHT MIRACLE

LIFE LESSONS

- Christians are drafted into the army of God upon conversion.
- Don't be moved by Satan's dirty tricks. God is still on the throne.
- God wants your family members saved, more than you do!

What shall we say to these things? If God be for us, who can be against us?

—ROMANS 8:31

WITH THE HORRIBLE tragedy of the September 11, 2001, terrorist attack came my absolute conviction of this being the End Times. I had already been experiencing my own attacks from the devil and his horde of demons. Now, as the entire world watched in fear, humanity couldn't comprehend the images flashing across their television screens. Horrific footage of civilian airplanes slamming into the Twin Towers was inconceivable.

How could anyone justify murdering thousands of innocent and unsuspecting lives? Such an act could only be explained as "the work of the devil," hypnotizing man-kind with crafty, irrational lies. At this isolated moment in time, evil was revealed for all to clearly see, and Christians (as well as the lost) were awakened to Satan's hatred for mankind. It was a sick feeling.

The devil comes to "kill, steal, and destroy" (John 10:10). His ruthless, vulgar, and unyielding tactics show no mercy. Satan's number one objective is to destroy families. He knows he can pervert nations once families are divided against one another.

And Jesus knew their thoughts, and said unto them, Every kingdom divided against itself is brought to desolation; and every city or house divided against itself shall not stand.

—MATTHEW 12:25

When it comes to protecting our families from the onslaught of hell's schemes, we must "gear up" daily by putting on the full armor of God. The powers of darkness are adamant in their plot to thwart God's plan. We must be just as determined to stand our ground against principalities and powers, not being moved by what we see or by what we feel. If you plan on being victorious in your quest for a Christian family made whole, mark your territory with the blood of Jesus, put on the full armor of God, and do all you know to do in the natural. Once you have exhausted yourself, by applying every spiritual and physical principle known, STAND YOUR GROUND. The battle is the Lord's!

> *Finally, my brethren, be strong in the Lord, and in the power of his might. Put on the whole armour of God, that ye may be able to stand against the wiles of the devil.*
>
> —EPHESIANS 6:10–11

I wish I could tell you that life is easy once you become a Christian, but unfortunately this is not at all the case. I will tell you that in spite of the trials and tribulations we all face, your life will be blessed when you keep it wrapped in the strong hand of Jesus. Our Father God has all confidence in our ability to overcome any situation. He calls us "more than conquerors" (Romans 8:37). The key to our success hinges on how well equipped we are with spiritual weapons *before* the enemy attacks (Ephesians 6:13–18).

Satan knows how to manipulate your mate into provoking your emotions. If your situation gets down and dirty, the way mine did, Satan will tempt you to become irrational and vindictive. He has been studying your personality, looking for a weak spot in your character since the day you were born. At an opportune moment in time, he strategically arranges situations and circumstances, carefully setting you up, to wreak havoc at your point of weakness; he wants to hit you where it hurts the most. Thinking you'll give up, his evil mirage is meant to make things "appear" as if they are too far gone even for God to repair.

> *There hath no temptation taken you but such as is common to man: but God is faithful, who will not suffer*

you to be tempted above that ye are able; but will with the temptation also make a way of escape, that ye may be able to bear it.
—1 CORINTHIANS 10:13

If you look around, you'll quickly see how the enemy of your soul uses the same ammunition on everyone. He comes up with nothing new. While we may feel as though we are the only ones suffering such shame and embarrassment, in reality, there are families all around going through similar trials; but, only those who fight with spiritual weapons, not carnal (physical) weapons, can expect to win the battle.

For though we walk in the flesh, we do not war after the flesh: (For the weapons of our warfare are not carnal, but mighty through God to the pulling down of strong holds).
—2 CORINTHIANS 10:3–4

As we take a look into how my story unfolds, this chapter reveals a defining moment in our family's journey to wholeness. The culmination of events that take place in this heartbreaking phase of "shakedown" prove to either claim victory or defeat for our marriage. Like it or not, the destiny of our family would be contingent upon "my response" to Satan's hardest hitting attack.

In my final phase of warfare over the salvation of my husband's soul and the wholeness of our family came the sobering reality of my need to go back to work—full time. It didn't make sense to me why God would have me sell my dance studios, just a few years earlier, only to place me in corporate America. Unfortunately, this was the path I was forced to embrace, as the waves of life came crashing down on our home. Still, deep in my heart, I knew this would only be necessary for a season; my Lord would deliver us soon!

*The LORD is my rock, and my fortress, and **my deliverer**; my God, my strength, in whom I will trust; my buckler, and the horn of my salvation, and my high tower.*
—PSALM 18:2, EMPHASIS ADDED

With God's favor, I was able to secure an extremely lucrative, corporate job in the modeling industry. My job title was Admissions Director, which is a fancy term to describe Sales Person. Upon my interview, I made it notably clear that I did not want to work nights and weekends. I was totally upfront with my faith and family values being prioritized as God, family, then business, and although hired in regard to my request, I suspect the owner was secretly plotting all along to change my mind. As it turned out, the position that I was hired to do could only be accomplished by my working nights and weekends! But, because I was desperate, and this job had a potentially enormous salary, I decided to "put my big girl pants on" and make the most of it for a season.

To further complicate my decision, I was placed under a supervisor who found great joy in making my life miserable. This man had no respect for families or God, and he was on a mission to strip me of mine. Pressing onward, I was determined to succeed in lieu of our family's financial crisis. I prayed without ceasing, "Lord, help me to accomplish the highest sales volume in the least amount of time. Oh, God, give me favor with the owner of this company so this job will become less stressful." In the most difficult of circumstances, I did my best to excel, never complaining about the dreadful behavior of my devilish supervisor. I had no choice.

God is so good! Within the first few months of my new job, my supervisor was fired, and you won't believe whom the Lord promoted to take his place—me! Instantly, my income tripled and my schedule eased up, just a little. This incredible salary increase was an answer to my prayer. By this point, my husband's sin had caused our finances to be near nonexistent, and this promotion was so instrumental in bailing our family out of ruin once again. For me to be newly employed (by corporate America) at the age of thirty-nine, without a college education and without prior experience—to earn more money than I had ever earned in my life—was truly amazing. My God is faithful; He is Jehovah Jireh—my provider!

And Abraham called the name of that place Jehovah-jireh: as it is said to this day, In the mount of the LORD it shall be seen.
—GENESIS 22:14

Before I actually sought out a full-time job (as led by the Lord), what I didn't realize was the "new cause" of our cursed land. You see, at the height of our financial nightmare and at the peak of our family's weakness arose a woman, sent by Satan, to finish us off, once and for all! My husband always said that he would never cheat on me. He and I were best friends; I know he truly loved me with all of his human heart. The problem is that humans are not capable of loving each other the way God intended, without the empowerment of the indwelling Holy Spirit. Consequently, when my husband was seduced by Satan's "whore," he had no willpower to withstand the intoxicating gestures from her cunning lure.

> For the lips of a strange woman drop as an honeycomb,
> and her mouth is smoother than oil: But her end is bitter
> as wormwood, sharp as a two-edged sword.
> —PROVERBS 5:3–4

Usually under the influence of alcohol, even during the day, my husband had no self-control. As his poor judgment was mixed with his "defeated mentality" (the "woe is me" syndrome), it created the justification he needed in his mind to cross that sacred line of fidelity in our marriage. After a monogamous seventeen-year relationship, my husband secretly entered into an adulterous affair with a woman he met at work. The moment he yielded to the devil's alluring ideas, breaking covenant with me and with God, the floodgates of hell opened up, and a host of demons invaded our home. Initially, I was blind to the root cause of our problems. The mastermind of hell had carefully plotted ways to cover what was really going on in our marriage; or perhaps, the Lord had put a veil over my eyes to protect me during this debilitating part of my journey.

In addition, once I became employed at my new corporate job, it became easier for my husband to sneak around. As I was scheduled to work late-night hours, along with weekends out of town, he was further freed up for more lewd behavior. Although I was very naïve during this time, there were a few moments when I sensed he might be cheating on me. But then, I would quickly disregard those thoughts, knowing I had been a loving and supporting wife through thick and thin. There was no way my husband would turn his back on me after I had shown so much grace throughout eleven years of disappointment, so I thought. I could feel spiritual wickedness in my home. I even saw images that I believe to be demons on occasion, but I did not connect the dots that clearly pointed toward adultery. This crime against me, our children, and even my husband's own body and soul went on for about nine months. All the while, I was unaware of the existence of another woman.

But then, one evening, while at work, I received a strange phone call from my husband. His voice was gruff, his words were short, and his emotions were void. He said, "The boys are being watched by a relative. I'll talk to you later"...*click*. He hung the phone up! I frantically tried to call him back, but there was no answer, no voice mail—nothing. What was going on? Something bad was happening. My heart began to race. I panicked!

As I rushed out the door from my job, I repeatedly dialed my husband's cell phone...over...and over...and over, again. Nothing! When I finally arrived home, I ran inside and picked up the house phone to try his number again. I hoped, "Maybe something was wrong with my cell phone; that's why I couldn't get his voice mail." As I picked up our home phone to dial out, I heard my husband's voice talking with this relative, so I quickly said, "Hey, Honey!" Again, *click*. He hung up the moment he heard my voice. My stomach sank! I leaped up the steps to find this family member on the couch in our game room. Pleading with him, I asked, "Where is my husband?"

Unfortunately, this relative did not use good judgment in his reply. He babbled some hideous response and changed the subject, in an attempt to make light of my situation. I screamed, "You just talked to my husband. Where is he? What is going on?"

As if I were the main character of a horror film, suddenly, everyone I loved and trusted was deceiving me. Again, he joked, "Oh, he'll be home soon. Go on to bed." Then, this family member walked out the door and left me with no answers. My boys were in bed asleep, upstairs. Sitting silently at my kitchen table, my world stopped. I tried to convince myself that my husband would be home at any minute. I tried not to panic. Nauseated, I watched the clock for an hour. It was 10:30 p.m.

Praying. Crying. Tormented. I was ashamed to make inquiring phone calls, because I didn't want to alarm anyone unnecessarily. Still hoping this was all a figment of my imagination, I didn't want to rock the boat by causing the community to raise their eyebrows, questioning my husband's character. Maybe he would walk through the door in just a minute and it would all be over. "Oh, God, *please!*"

After waiting several hours alone, I called my relative and demanded that he tell me where my husband was. As I woke him from a deep sleep, his unconcerned reply didn't set well with me. Patronizing me, he said, "He's probably out with the guys. He'll be home later. Go on to bed and stop calling me. It's late." My husband had *never* left me in suspense over his whereabouts. We had been married for almost eighteen years, and I had never experienced anything like this night before. I knew something was terribly wrong, and I was growing increasingly angry with this relative, as his apathy toward my cries for help only added salt to my wounds. It didn't make any sense to me that a close relative would not be concerned about the location of a missing family member. He knew something, and I was determined to find out what it was.

Well, I called this relative every hour—on the hour—and asked the same question over and over, "Where is my husband?"

Each time I called, my voice became more demanding than the time before. Still, he had no sympathy and did not seem alarmed that my husband was missing. When he finally said, "I wouldn't lie to you, I'm a Christian," the very core of my faith was shaken. How could anyone blatantly lie, while adding to their lie, "I am a Christian?" I could hear all of hell laughing behind a masquerade of gestures. This was a living nightmare.

Eventually, I called my mom—which I hated to do, especially at 3:00 a.m. I didn't want her to know the extent of our troubles. I knew she was already worried sick about the well being of our family because she and my step-father had come to our rescue on several occasions throughout our financial traumas. She had watched my heart break many times over the past few years, and I knew her patience would grow thin with my husband once she found out that he had abandoned me and the boys. Just the same, I had to seek some type of solace for my mind, and I didn't know whom else to call. She tried to comfort me and said she would come over right away, but I told her to wait. I was still hoping that my husband would be home at any minute, and I didn't want to have a house full of people when he arrived.

My next call was to the police. I rationalized, "My husband could be hurt." Getting them to put out an APB for him took some convincing because the police department does not usually issue an APB until someone has been missing for twenty-four hours. Finally, they agreed to send an officer over to my house. He arrived at around 4:00 that morning. I had been up all night crying.

The enemy is a master at setting people up for failure. As I opened the door, expecting some bald, overweight, grumbling old policeman, I was instead greeted by a middle-aged officer, who looked like he just stepped off the pages of *GQ Magazine*. Here I am feeling sorry for myself, thinking my husband just left me for another woman, and up walks this uniformed "superman" to console me. The devil wanted me to take my eyes off of the prize (victory in Jesus) to focus on the possibility of finding someone new. He even had this officer tell me my husband was just prowling around. He said, "This kind of thing happens all the time. He'll be home in the morning."

After the initial shock subsided (sitting in my nightgown, alone with a strange man, who looked like a hero), the Holy Spirit prompted me to refocus on the fact that God had not called me to a life of fantasy. He has called me to a life of victory and righteousness! I was determined to find my husband. Still hoping he had a great explanation for his disappearance and praying this night would be accounted for with relief, I filled out the report.

As the night became morning, I sat in a hellish silence. My desolate thoughts haunted me. I hadn't slept a wink, and my tired body was paralyzed from depression. As the sun began to rise, I knew my life had just taken a turn for the worst. For the first time in eighteen years of marriage, my husband had stayed out all night, unannounced! I concluded our marriage was defiled.

As my children crawled out of bed and began to ask, "Where is Daddy?" I saw their little hearts melt in anguish. They tried to comfort me with their sweet hugs of affection, but they too, did not have words to express the void and confusion that filled our home.

In that moment, I began to think back upon my childhood. I remembered the emptiness I felt as my mom and dad made vows of divorce after violent arguments. Recalling the despondent emotions and confused thoughts of a scared nine-year-old little girl, I relived the day my mom and I packed up a U-Haul to leave my dad, that final time. I always said, "I would never get a divorce," and yet, here I was, headed down the same road that my parents had traveled thirty years earlier. Somehow, even in my careful calculations and God-centered approach to marriage, the devil managed to penetrate my prayer wall. (I would later learn how this generational curse slipped through the cracks and how my response to this situation held the key to the outcome.) Now, my children's future was at stake. It seemed everything I had ever believed about my life, as a Christian, was placed before me in this valley of decision.

At 8:00 a.m., the sound of the telephone ringing pierced my gut with fear. In a trance, I picked up the phone to hear the voice of my husband. Not knowing whether I should be happy or sad, I listened intently as he began to speak. I could hear the anxiety in his voice as he whispered to me, "Get in a room where the children can't hear you. Lock the door. I need to tell you something."

In dire need to be comforted, while bracing for loneliness, I locked myself in our bedroom and melted into a deep groan as he confessed his sin—all of it. I wanted these words to go away. I begged him to, "Please, take it back!" Adultery was the one sin that carried implications of our marriage being over. I wasn't willing to accept losing my husband forever, and so I just screamed a silent, gut-wrenching wail as I listened to his confession and pleas for forgiveness.

I remember asking, "Why, why, why?" I screamed, "You are headed straight for hell!" Questions poured out of my mouth: "How could you turn your back on me when all I ever did was love you? If you fell into sin with this woman at a moment of weakness, how could you go back for more—for nine months—that's almost a year! How could you make love to me and then have sex with her? Did you not think about our children? Did you not think about sexual diseases? Did you not consider the fact that her husband might have killed you? You could have AIDS! Oh, my God, I could have AIDS!" I was hysterical! For the first time in my entire life, I thought I was losing my mind. A whirlwind of debilitating thoughts flooded my head on that morning of doom; it was only the beginning of my fight for sanity. The next year of my life would be a time of taking thoughts captive in a way I had never imagined possible. "God, please help me! Help me, Lord!" I prayed.

> *Casting down imaginations, and every thing that exalteth itself against the knowledge of God, and bringing into captivity every thought to the obedience of Christ.*
> —2 CORINTHIANS 10:5

Shortly after I hung up the phone, my youngest son said to me, "Mommy, does this mean you and Daddy will be getting a divorce?" My son's words rang into every cavity of my being as I was faced with the hardest choice I ever had to make. A thousand thoughts filled my mind as I considered both divorce and fighting for my marriage. I don't remember exactly what I told my son, but I think I said, "I don't know."

> *I call heaven and earth to record this day against you, that I have set before you life and death, blessing and cursing: therefore choose life, that both thou and thy seed may live.*
> —DEUTERONOMY 30:19

The next thing I remember happening was my mother and one of my sister's friends coming to my home, trying to comfort me. I just sat, lifeless, as they took care of my children, working to keep a pleasant atmosphere—for them. I remember my sister's friend telling me, "You need to have the locks changed." In agreement, I sat like a zombie as they called the locksmith. I really can't tell you much about what happened that morning. Things were going on around me, but I was sitting still.

To add to my torment, I was scheduled to go to work at 1:00 p.m. that day. This particular day was the most important one of the week for salespeople, and our family really needed the money. Somehow, I managed to get myself dressed and headed out the door—as if I were going to be able to work. Driving toward my job, my heart was crying out to the Lord for help. I needed help in getting my mind to function normally. The resounding voice of the "spirit of fear," along with the overwhelming gloom of "the dregs of despair," joined forces in unison, chanting words of discouragement faster than I could cast them down. In the middle of this chaos, I found myself taking a detour that led to our church. I had to see a man of God, someone that could speak life back into me. I was perishing for a drink of "cold, living water," and I felt my thirst could only be satisfied by going to the house of the Lord.

When I walked into the church office, the receptionist asked, "Who are you here to see?" I collapsed in the lobby and sobbed. She quickly called for a pastor, gave me some tissues, and sat in silent prayer, waiting for my help to arrive.

The pastor that was available to see me, along with his female assistant, listened to my mental, emotional, and spiritual breakdown and then *gently* began to offer very compassionate encouragement, according to God's Word. Upon regaining my composure, they prayed over me and challenged me to be strong for my children. They advised me to pray diligently before making any final decisions concerning my marriage. They also prayed for my husband.

> *Have not I commanded thee? Be strong and of a good courage; be not afraid, neither be thou dismayed: for the* LORD *thy God is with thee withersoever thou goest.*
> —JOSHUA 1:9

I left the church office and went on to work. I felt obligated to tell my supervisor what had transpired and how I, regretfully, could not stay for work. My supervisor was very understanding, and in trying to offer words of encouragement, she actually caused my heart to sink even further into despair. You see, my supervisor was once married to the "love of her life," but when the same thing happened to her, they split. This supervisor was now in her 50s, still single, and very bitter. The devil was saying to me, "This is your future." The devil is a liar!

This dark day of death in the life of my marriage was on a Thursday. My husband and I talked on the phone several times between that Thursday morning and the next Saturday night, but I made no plans to let him in the house. Then, on Saturday night he asked me if I would pick him up on the way to church the next day. "Sure," I thought. "Whatever." I picked him up from his dad's house, and the four of us—me, him, and the children—headed out to the 11:00 worship service.

Recalling those three days in our marriage, as being parallel to Jesus' death, burial, and resurrection; it was when the darkest day of our life collided with the best day of our life, and the three days of suspense in between those two days, seemed like the end. God used my three-day experience to reveal how the disciples, Jesus' mother, and all of His followers must have felt as they watched the Son of God being crucified. It made no sense to them how such vile acts could be carried out on the one they believed to be the Creator of the universe. I am sure they had moments, probably three days, of confusion. The devil must have made them feel like fools, during those three days, as Jesus lay lifeless in a borrowed tomb. Praise God, that's not the end of the story!

I have never wailed so much throughout an entire church service as I did on this day. Even though we were members of a Pentecostal church, our worship services were not always reminiscent of typical Pentecostal expressions. Most of our church services were fairly traditional in format. This particular Sunday, however, the Spirit of the Lord was stirring among His people and, for me, it was perfect timing! I cried out loud and worshiped God like never before. My acutely distraught cries blended into the congregational worship, yet stood out with a pain and agony that carried a distinct sound from the others. (We later purchased a CD of this church service and relived that defining moment. As my husband pointed out vaguely hearing me above the crowd, tears rolled down his cheeks.)

After praise and worship, I got control of myself long enough to hear the message being preached. It wasn't surprising that the Lord had that pastor preach the strongest salvation message that I have ever heard. At the end of the message—but before the official altar call—my husband ran down front, crying out to the Lord. I had prayed for twelve long years for this moment to become a reality, but because of my broken heart, I now felt no joy in what was happening. Instead, I paced the church praying someone would comfort me in my pain.

Since I was a former choir member, I ran to the choir room hoping to find a friend. When I got there, I was shocked to see a room full of strangers where, much to my surprise, the church had used this space for the overflow attendance during this particular service. So in desperation, I wandered back into the sanctuary and fell on the opposite side of the altar from where my husband had knelt. Sobbing profusely, I cried out to God saying, "Lord, I will not get up, until you tell me what my next move is!" Two hours later, I was able to stand to my feet as some precious ladies, who had stayed praying over me the entire time, spoke prophetic words of encouragement into my spirit. On the other side of the altar were godly men who stood praying, rebuking, and commanding demons to leave my husband. I didn't even think about my precious children, but thankfully, someone at the church made sure they were well taken care of.

I made a choice at the altar that day to fight for my marriage. I did not get up feeling like a new woman; in fact, when I got up, I felt just as frightened as when I knelt down. But even so, the Holy Spirit of God overshadowed me and empowered me to face my troubles with a more-than-conqueror attitude.

One of those sweet, godly women got in my face and said, "Don't think about the pain you feel right now. Instead, think about the future. Look at your husband. He says he is truly sorry for the things he has done. He says he just received Christ as his Lord and Savior. If he is telling the truth, he is a new man. Begin to think of future Christmases with your unborn grandchildren. Think about the wonderful long life that extends far beyond this short season of pain. Think of growing old together, sitting in your rocking chairs, holding hands. This part of your life will seem so small in those final years."

I could smell her breath as she pressed her forehead against my bowed head. As tears ran down her face, her words of exhortation were bold and sincere. I had no confidence to lift my head and look at her face, but I did notice she had on nice shoes. I later realized God had used a very prominent woman of influence to minister to me. This was all part of His perfect plan—as I was so downtrodden financially, spiritually, physically, emotionally, and every other way imaginable. Strangely, her willingness to minister to me—a woman who didn't have two nickels to rub together—gave me hope. God used her stature as a mirrored reflection of His promise to even restore our finances. The details of God's love amaze me!

I'll be honest. Her words were bouncing off of me like ping-pong balls. I wasn't sure if I could get past my pain. Even so, her picturesque words became the very foundation for every decision I made—from that day forward.

My husband truly got up from the altar a new creature (2 Corinthians 5:17). He was gloriously born again and set free from all addictions from that moment on. Everything from cigarettes, alcohol, pornography, gambling—all gone! My husband had a new heart (and a new mind), and, miraculously, he was now equipped by the power of the Holy Spirit to handle my emotional wounds—wounds that would only be healed with time. Thank you, Jesus!

> *But he was wounded for our transgressions, he was bruised for our iniquities: the chastisement of our peace was upon him; and with his stripes we are healed.*
> —ISAIAH 53:5

LIFE APPLICATION

God promises us that no plague will come near our dwelling. He promises to be a deliverer for those who abide in His presence. Meditate on Psalm 91 and ask the Lord to speak to you concerning your marital situation.

eight

THE TRUTH THAT SETS US FREE

LIFE LESSONS

- The devil's greatest deception is religion. People who "think" they are right with God have no need for a Savior.
- Seeing our mate through the eyes of Jesus involves recognizing truth and then administering compassion.
- God wants people whole. The devil wants people patched.

And ye shall know the truth, and the
truth shall make you free.

—JOHN 8:32

HOW DOES GOD DEFINE *MARRIAGE*?

And He answered and said unto them, Have ye not read, that he which made them at the beginning made

> *them male and female, And said, For this cause shall*
> *a man leave father and mother, and shall cleave to his*
> *wife: and they twain shall be one flesh? Wherefore they*
> *are no more twain, but one flesh. What therefore God*
> *hath joined together, let not man put asunder.*
>
> —MATTHEW 19:4–6

Even though my spirit desperately wanted to stay married, my soul (mind, will, and emotions) was screaming out, "Divorce!" Wrestling to take thoughts captive—and feeling as though I were hanging onto my faith merely by the last joint of my pinky finger—the "spirit of fear" worked overtime seeking to consume me. How could the future of my home now rest upon *my* decision of whether to stay married or not? This seemed to be an unfair judgment placed in my lap, seeing how I was the victim of something I had nothing to do with. I felt I had made a choice to be married, eighteen years earlier, when I said, "I do," and now—somehow—being forced to choose whether I should stay married or get a divorce frustrated me to the point of mental agony. I wanted to stay married because I loved my husband! But oh, how my heart bled, as my mind unwillingly flipped from one scenario to another. I cried, "Lord, please make my mind stop!"

Before everything fell apart, I had been looking toward my calling. I knew, early on that God wanted me to be "all His," and I knew He had a special plan for me in ministry. Now, I was finding it hard to believe His plan would include me being a divorced, single mom.

Torn and confused, I began to selfishly seek God's Word for grounds permitting divorce; but, much to my surprise, I discovered a truth that actually helped me to focus on staying married.

*They say unto him, Why did Moses then command to give a writing of divorcement, and to put her [or him] away? He saith unto them, Moses **because of the hardness of your hearts** suffered you to put away your wives [or husbands]: but from the beginning it was not so.*

—MATTHEW 19:7–8, EMPHASIS ADDED

As I pondered the reply Jesus gave the Pharisees when they asked, "Why did Moses then command to give a writing of divorcement...?" I discovered it was only granted because of the "hardness of the people's hearts." Ouch! This means the Lord wants us to remain married, even in the case of adultery—if we can get our hearts to line up with His heart. I did not want to have a "hard heart"! I had spent the past twelve years cultivating a soft and compassionate heart in Christ, and now, as this life-sized bitter pill was forced down my throat, I desperately wanted to be freed from its poison! But how?

Create in me a clean heart, O God; and renew a right spirit within me.

—PSALM 51:10

In the Old Testament law given to Moses, God does not label the one who has been betrayed as an adulterer—if they divorce and remarry. He has great compassion on those the enemy has exploited and offers a way of escape for those who are not strong enough to press on. God understands the mental torment that human beings go through from such deep wounds; the pain and agony caused by infidelity. Thus, divorce is allowed, but it is not God's perfect plan.

On the other hand, the Lord knows the great rewards that await those who are willing to persevere through this terribly tough time. It is only by allowing the Holy Spirit to prove Himself strong on our behalf that we can experience the abundant life God has for us. This means we will have to get out of our boat of fairytale comfort in order to walk on the crashing waves of real-life experiences, all the while keeping our eyes firmly fixed on Jesus. Although in the natural realm this seems to be an impossible assignment in the wake of infidelity, in the spiritual realm it is the only way to inherit the fullness of God's miraculous blessings.

> *And he said, Come. And when Peter was come down out of the ship, he walked on the water, to go to Jesus.*
> —MATTHEW 14:29

After a lot of prayer, I came to realize the following principles as being more important to me than my personal happiness:

- I wanted my God to be glorified.

- I wanted my children to be spared from a life of brokenness and confusion.

- I wanted to hear my Lord say, "Well done, thou good and faithful servant" (Matthew 25:21).

The scripture verse I claimed to remind myself of my declaration was Galatians 2:20.

> *I am crucified with Christ: nevertheless I live: yet not I, but Christ liveth in me: and the life which I now live in*

the flesh I live by the faith of the Son of God, who loved me, and gave himself for me.

—GALATIANS 2:20

As weird as this may sound, this season of my being painfully crucified with Christ brought me to identify with "cutters." The excruciating pain in my spirit can only be described as one bleeding. Whenever my mind would want to retaliate with vengeance (and it was a daily thought until my complete healing manifested nine months later), my soul would bleed—spiritually speaking—as I forced myself to obey God, restraining the flesh from taking matters into its own hands. Please don't take this out of context; I would never cut myself physically, and I pray none of you would ever consider such irrational behavior. I am simply saying that I now understand the severe emotional pain of those suffering from this disorder. With compassion, I can honestly say, "Jesus will set you free once and for all!" Just ask Him, and keep on asking, until your healing becomes a reality.

I say unto you, though he will not rise and give him, because he is his friend, yet because of his importunity [persistence] he will rise and give him as many as he needeth.

—LUKE 11:8

By now, I am well aware that some of you reading this book have conjured up many differences between my testimony and "your situation." The enemy is trying his best to convince you, "It may not be right for you to stay married to your husband."

Some of you may be arguing, "But, my husband has not become a Christian since his adulterous lifestyle has been exposed." Many of you are thinking, "Yeah, but my husband is a Christian, so how can I ever reconcile to a man who has turned on me and on God in such a vile and deceitful way?" Still, others are wondering, "But, my husband has not committed adultery, he just drinks all the time." Or, "He only has a problem with _____" (you fill in the blank).

HE'S NOT A CHRISTIAN

Let's start with those of you whose husbands have admittedly not become a Christian since their sin was exposed. Just because the timing of your testimony is different from mine, does not conclude God's will as being divorce. You've heard the saying, "It's not over—until the fat lady sings." I like to say, "It's not over—until death do us part." When the two of you said your vows on your wedding day, you promised each other, before the Lord, that you would be bound together, "For better, for worse—for richer, for poorer—in sickness and in health." Now that you are living through the worse, poorer, or sickness part of your marriage covenant, consider it to be a "test" of your commitment!

You could very well be the one person God wants to use in bringing about salvation for your husband. What an honor to think, the Lord trusts you enough to nurture the eternal destiny of your spouse. As in Esther 4:14, you may have been born "for such a time as this." Many of you will never go on a foreign mission, and most may not serve in full-time ministry, but everyone has a mission field, and it's called *the home*! Just remember, there is nothing too hard for God (Jeremiah 32:17). Continue to seek the Lord on how to demonstrate "agape love" toward your husband, even during the most painful of times. First Corinthians 13:8 says, "Love never fails." I believe God's Word! I believe the love of Jesus pouring out of your brokenness will not fail to bring about a softening of your husband's heart, leaving him vulnerable and ready to repent.

Very important: If you are still praying for your husband's salvation, be sure to bind salvation to his forehead, to his heart, to his hands, and feet. Do this according to Deuteronomy 6:8. Also, cover him in the blood of Jesus daily. Regardless of the sinful lifestyle he is currently participating in, you are in covenant relationship with your husband, according to God's Word, and the Lord takes covenant relationships very seriously. When the Israelites smeared the blood of the sacrificial lamb over the doorposts of their homes, everyone in the home was saved (Exodus 12). This same act of obedience works for us today as New Testament believers. We should claim the blood of Jesus over the doors of our homes, so when the death angel passes by, everyone will be saved; the death angel in this case—being the demon of divorce.

HE IS A CHRISTIAN

Some of you are plagued with leery thoughts, "But, my husband was a pastor (or some other ministry worker) before all of this happened. I just don't think I could ever trust him again." I believe this is the toughest group in ministering reconciliation to, because there seems to be nothing for them to hang future trust on. The points I am about to make may seem radically foreign at first, but I pray you'll search God's Word carefully and take into consideration the fruit of your mate's character prior to his fall before discounting my theory.

But the fruit of the Spirit is love, joy, peace, longsuf-fering, gentleness, goodness, faith, meekness, temperance [self control]: against such there is no law.

—GALATIANS 5:22–23

Remember, the devil is a master deceiver. He would want you to *think* your husband's heart was right before the Lord, when he made the choice to betray you. (By the way, most likely he didn't "accidentally" end up in bed with another woman; he made a decision to sin.) Without knowing your husband person-ally, I would say (possibly) your husband somehow followed after a calling before he first truly committed his whole heart to Christ. Go back and study the parable of the wheat and the tares (Matthew 13). There are so many scriptures in God's Word about, what I call, "counterfeit Christians."

He that saith, I know him, and keepeth not his command-ments, is a liar, and the truth is not in him.

—1 JOHN 2:4

Yet, for some reason the New Testament church today, as a whole, tries to act as though Christians are just stumbling into adultery by the droves. We need to stop thinking like an infidel and start thinking like the Spirit of the Lord. God is holy and He is coming back for a church without spot, blemish, or wrinkle (Ephesians 5:27). Personally, I think it is a great relief to acknowledge someone as being an impostor. Once the truth is exposed, healing can begin! God is not in the business of putting Band-Aids or masks on people, He is in the business of making people whole. It is a lot easier to make sense out of this ugly mess once you understand that a sinner sins. They can't help themselves. Is it possible that your husband had a "form of godliness, but denied the power thereof" (2 Timothy 3:5).

Ever learning, and never able to come to the knowledge of the truth.

—2 Timothy 3:7

There are some people who ended up in ministry because they came from a family of ministers. While it is a wonderful thing to boast of generation after generation in professional Christian ministry, it is likely there are some who enter into ministry as a career and not as a calling.

Then, there are some adults who are still living in the faith of their parents. In this case, an adult grew up in a Christian home and maybe even went to Christian school. They may have adopted their parents' faith in the same way we adopt a political party or patriotic citizenship. Perhaps your husband has never made Jesus his personal Lord (his Master). Could it be feasible he never had an opportunity to be tested in his Christian walk, and now that the test has presented itself, he failed—because he only had his parents' faith?

Another way of looking at it is that your husband has been much like Judas, in that he has been following Jesus and his teachings for a number of years, but yet held darkness in his heart throughout his entire journey. John 3:19 tells us, "The light has come into the world, and people loved darkness rather than the light because their deeds were evil." Judas never truly repented of his greed. Maybe your husband never truly repented of his lust. Everyone has a weakness. Satan "seeks whom he may devour" by looking for that weak spot in an individual's life (1 Peter 5:8). If it were not for the blood of Jesus covering your weaknesses, who's to say you would not have done the same thing, if given the right circumstances and carefully calculated timing?

Whatever the reason, the good news is that the Word of God does not return void (Isaiah 55:11). The Lord will cause every scripture your husband ever knew to come alive and prosper, once he has repented of his pride and arrogance as a minister of the gospel who failed to do things in order. Your job is to persevere. I know this is horribly painful right now, but once the tests have been passed (Test #1—for you to forgive; Test #2—for your husband to repent), your life will take on a completely new joy—your marriage will be born again! You will truly live in the kingdom of God on earth!

I believe a person who is truly born again has insurance against following after a sinful lifestyle. If we have truly given our whole heart to the Lord, and we are staying in God's Word, the Holy Spirit will not allow us to wallow in sin as the world does. Besides, there is a "sin unto death" (Romans 6:16; 1 John 5:16). While we don't know for sure what this sin is in the life of an individual, I, personally, don't believe that the Lord would allow a true man of God to destroy the lives of so many people (the church family and his personal family), making a mockery of the death of His Son, Jesus, without taking him on home to glory.

> *For if we sin wilfully after that we have received the knowledge of the truth, there remaineth no more sacrifice for sins.*
>
> —HEBREWS 10:26

Of how much sorer punishment, suppose ye, shall he be thought worthy, who hath trodden under foot the Son of God, and hath counted the blood of the covenant, wherewith he was sanctified, an unholy thing, and hath done despite unto the Spirit of grace?

—HEBREWS 10:29

The Lord's mercy and grace are to bring about repentance for the sinner and to cultivate growth in the Christian life, not to allow a born-again, blood-bought child of God a license to willfully live a lifestyle of sin. In fact, the Word of God says, "We should not frustrate the grace of God" (Galatians 2:21). To think that the blood of Jesus can heal the sick and raise the dead, yet it cannot stop a person from committing adultery is blasphemy. The Bible says blasphemy against the Holy Spirit is not forgiven (Matthew 12:31).

Or despisest thou the riches of his goodness and forbear-ance and longsuffering; not knowing that the goodness of God leadeth thee to repentance?

—ROMANS 2:4

I know, some of you are saying, "But, what about King David?" King David lived under the Old Covenant, and even though he was a man after God's own heart, he was not a blood-bought, born-again, New Testament Christian. King David sinned against God, and consequently, he paid a very heavy price for his sin. Romans 6:23 tells us, "The wages of sin is death." David's sin with Bathsheba brought about death in his household, and this is certainly not something that should be taken lightly in the mind of the believer. We should learn from David's mistakes, emphasizing the importance of walking in obedience to the Holy Spirit.

> *Now therefore the sword shall never depart from thine house; because thou hast despised me, and hast taken the wife of Uriah the Hittite to be thy wife.*
>
> —2 SAMUEL 12:10

Today, the New Covenant Christian has been divinely made a new creature, in which old things have passed away and all things have become new (2 Corinthians 5:17). The scriptures tell us, plainly, that the same Spirit who raised Christ from the dead now lives on the inside of every born-again, new covenant believer (Romans 8:11). Stop and think about that for a moment! Meditate on how much spiritual power and authority it took for God to change the laws of gravity and the laws of death, in order for His Son to be raised from the dead. That same power— according to God's Word—lives on the inside of every child of God. Wow! That not only means power for someone to avoid a sinful lifestyle, but it also means power to forgive.

I have personally known three different preachers who walked into the sin of adultery. One of them actually committed sodomy (adultery with the same sex) against his wife and five children. I always thought there was something shady about these men and their ministry, but I could not put my finger on it. Most church people never saw it coming because they were looking at mannerisms, methods, and behavior patterns with natural eyes, not spiritual eyes. I bet if the truth were known, these former wives would have some insight about the character of these men, behind closed doors.

Only God knows the heart of a person, so for you to take for granted that a title or a persona means a person is "who they say they are" is foolish. We can only judge by the fruit of a person what might be buried deep within. I have even found that counterfeit Christians can manifest some evidence of fruit, even though they are not born again. I say this, not to cause you to be a skeptic about other Christians, but rather, to help you avoid being deceived time and time again. We should put all of our trust and faith in the Lord and not in man. Whatever others do is between them and God. Try to bring this thinking into your marriage; it will help you trust the Lord for the victory.

I really feel sorry for these fallen preachers and fallen Christian impostors because they know the scriptures. In Hebrews 6:4–6 the Bible says it is impossible to renew these fallen men unto repentance because this would mean they'd have to crucify Jesus all over again. If these people believe they are Christians, they'll find it very difficult to get past this and many other scriptures, in order to be reconciled to the Lord. This is probably why the three preachers I once knew are still living in sin today. Sadly, their families are destroyed, and their children are severely scarred—spiritually, emotionally, and physically.

> *For it is impossible for those who were once enlightened, and have tasted of the heavenly gift, and were made partakers of the Holy Ghost, And have tasted the good word of God, and the powers of the world to come, If they shall fall away, to renew them again unto repentance;*

seeing they crucify to themselves the Son of God afresh, and put him to an open shame.

—HEBREWS 6:4–6

The Bible says we should know the truth and the truth shall set us free (John 8:32). I think this passage not only refers to the truth of God's Word setting us free, but also to the truth of one's soul. As long as people hide behind their "traditions of men" and "doctrines of devils," the truth will never be revealed, and it will plunge individuals into an eternal hell unknowingly (Mark 7:8). I say, "God, show us the truth about ourselves and about others you have sent to us for ministry so we can come to repentance, living in right-standing with the Holy God of the universe. Help us to utilize spiritual gifts such as a word of knowledge or the gift of discernment so we may be able to determine, pray, and act upon the truth" (1 Corinthians 12:8).

HE JUST SINS WITH _____?

For those of you who don't think your husband has committed adultery, the information within this chapter still applies to you—if you want to win the battle! All lifestyles of darkness are against God and His kingdom. We shouldn't expect to get a breakthrough miracle unless we are willing to spiritually attack the root of our problems. An example would be a wife praying for her husband to quit drinking when the root cause of his addiction is his salvation. God's Word says, "You have not, because you ask not" (James 4:2); and then it goes on to say that when you do ask, you miss the point (James 4:3). The Lord wants people to be whole. The word *salvation* actually means to make something whole; this is not just for eternity but also for the life we live now (1 Timothy 4:8). Hallelujah!

BORN AGAIN/COUNTERFEIT?

I believe once you are truly saved, you are saved forever (John 10:29; Ephesians 1:13). The problem is when someone we know has an emotional moment of tears and a genuine fear of going to hell, and then some other Christian tells them they are now saved. Only that person and the Lord know the truth of the matter. If the person who prayed and cried never shows fruit of being born again, then according to scripture, they are not. My husband was baptized at age thirteen, but he did not become a born again Christian until he was thirty-nine. Likewise, I said the sinner's prayer as a child, and then again many times as a teen, but I did not repent of my sin and make Jesus the Lord of my life until I was in my late twenties.

Sure, people who are born-again are capable of sinning unwillfully. They are also capable of sinning willfully "for a moment." The difference is that a true born-again believer does not practice sin. Not only that, the Bible says once you are born again, the laws of God are written on your heart. One of God's laws is, "Thou shalt not commit adultery." Adultery against a loving spouse is, in my opinion, the same as "murder" because you kill your spouse when you betray them in this most destructive of all sins. Then, once you have committed adultery and spiritual murder, you'll have to lie in order to cover your sin. So now you have gone against the laws written on your heart not once, but three times! I choose to believe that my faith in the death, burial, and resurrection of Jesus Christ is more powerful than such pernicious sinful behavior. After all, Jesus saved me from my sinful lifestyle, and He keeps me from going back into darkness on a daily basis. My heart is just as wicked as anyone else's, so I feel confident that what salvation does for me, it will do for everyone (Acts 10:34). The Word also tells us, whom the Lord loves, He chastens (Proverbs 3:11), and I am quite sure that Abba God is very capable of keeping His children in line.

I have met a few couples that claim the husband was a Christian before the adultery, saying he fell into sin. Somehow, these precious wives have been able to accept this as being the truth, and these couples appear to be doing great. I still believe there is an element of pride in these men because they do not admit they were not right with God all along. I think their testimony is dangerous for the ears of their children, for other "would be" Christians and for those contemplating adultery, because it leaves an open door of opportunity to sin. If the devil can just get his foot in the door of a person's heart, he can destroy them! If these men don't humble themselves to admit they were not right with the Lord before they sinned against their family, I fear it will be very difficult for the children of these men to fully understand the power of the gospel when their own father couldn't even be tamed by the Holy Spirit.

In Isaiah 53:5, the Bible tells us, "He was bruised for our iniquities." Again in Titus 2:14 we read Jesus died to redeem us of all iniquity. The word *iniquity* in Hebrew means a perversity, a moral evil, and mischief. In the Greek, this word means transgression of the law or a violation of the law. It also means unrighteousness. To put it simply, a person's iniquity causes him or her to be bent toward specific sins, repetitively. The person is wired to sin habitually with no strength to overcome the lure of sin's power. Jesus paid the price for our iniquity. He broke the bondage of sin, once and for all!

Now I know there is a doctrine that uses the words of Paul to justify a person's problem with sin. Many teach that because Paul says the things he wants to do, he doesn't, and the things he doesn't want to do, he does; this is grounds for saying, "I am a weak Christian." I think they are taking Paul's words out of context to create an opening for an occasion to sin. Perhaps some church leaders are uncomfortable telling church members the truth, once their sin has been exposed. The Bible says we will know them (true believers) by their fruit. If there is bad fruit, there is a bad root!

I have given you all of this information about sin because I want you to see your husband the way that Jesus sees him! Human beings do not know the true condition of another's heart; only the Lord can see the inward parts of a person. It is possible the devil has deceived you and your spouse for many years about the true condition of your spouse's heart. This would insure Satan of a sure win in the destruction of your family, and if this deception were left unchecked and not dealt with, it would thrust your husband into an eternal separation from God at the judgment. Praise God, if the truth has been exposed. Now pray for the Lord to *save your husband!*

> *Many will say to me in that day, Lord, Lord, have we not prophesied in thy name? and in thy name have cast out devils? and in thy name done many wonderful works?*

And then will I profess unto them, I never knew you: depart from me, ye that work iniquity.

—MATTHEW 7:22–23

I want you to see your husband through the eyes of Jesus. If you are convinced he is a man of God who chose to betray you, the church, and even His Lord, it will be very difficult to get past your pain and bitterness. You must see your husband as a sinner, in need of redemption. Then, once your husband has repented of his sins, ask God to help you forgive and forget— the way Jesus does!

This brings me to the next part of my journey—forgiveness. This is the hardest part.

LIFE APPLICATION

Study Luke 11:1–28 to understand more about prayer, persistence (importunity), God's goodness, deliverance, and the importance of keeping God's Word.

The Lord wants us to be whole, but we must be willing to face the root of our problem if we expect to receive His deliverance.

nine

FORGIVENESS IS A COMMANDMENT

LIFE LESSONS

- Regardless of the offence, God commands us to forgive and forget.
- It only takes a very small amount of faith (mustard seed faith) to be victorious in God's kingdom.
- It's impossible to stay mad at someone when you are praying for him or her.

And be kind one to another, tenderhearted, forgiving one another, even as God for Christ's sake hath forgiven you.

—EPHESIANS 4:32

THREE DAYS LATER...ON June 2, 2002, upon leaving church that Sunday, I allowed my husband back into our home for the first time since his disappearing act. We talked for hours about deep issues within each of our hearts, disclosing secret childhood wounds, insecurities, weaknesses, fears, and needs. This bittersweet, yet somehow romantic, communion was more intimate than all of our eighteen previous years of conversation combined. Although this proved to be "resurrection day," our marriage was far from being restored. I had a long way to go in learning to trust again. The process of forgiveness would take time—a lot of time!

While my husband had truly given his heart to Jesus that day, I, on the other hand, felt lost. It was quite a twist. I had been on fire for the Lord for twelve years and now, suddenly, emptiness was flooding my entire being. I was a dead woman. For the first time in my life, I couldn't find my faith, my vision was gone (spiritually speaking), and all zeal for life was snuffed out. I wondered, "Would I ever be the same again?" I was a mess.

Yes, I had made a decision at the altar that day to fight for my marriage, but I had no idea just how hard it would be to fight my own flesh. Bitterness is a disease; it is a slow and silent killer. While my intentions were to forgive my husband and reconcile our marriage, my soul (mind, will, and emotions) challenged my spirit. There was a war going on inside of me. I was tempted to retaliate with hate and violence, to seek sexual satisfaction outside of our marriage (to prove I was desirable), to drink, to curse, to smoke, and to *quit!* The devil had prepared a lewd party, and all of hell's demons were invited to throw darts of temptation at me, as the scheming hordes of hell were certain it wouldn't take much to annihilate me—once and for all. I kept asking God, "How did I wind up in hell on earth, when all I ever wanted was to serve You?" If it were possible for one to lose their salvation, I would have certainly lost mine during this time.

Another twisted scheme from the devil's den was the temptation of lust. So many times during this trial I would receive complements from strange men. In all of my life, I don't think I have ever been more attractive than during this season of feeling so ugly. I felt as though I had a tag on my back that read, "I need love. I'm single. Do you think I'm pretty?" At my weakest moment, the enemy of my soul made sure I was tempted in every way possible. My flesh was screaming, "Feed me! Let me have the satisfaction of feeling sexy. I deserve it!" At first, the temptations were a challenge, but once I caught onto the devil's manipulation, I could more easily cast these vain imaginations down.

> *Watch and pray, that ye enter not into temptation: the spirit indeed is willing, but the flesh is weak.*
> —MATTHEW 26:41

Regretfully, I did have several moments of hating, hitting, smoking, drinking, and cursing. The Holy Spirit would convict me throughout each outburst, challenging me to get control of myself, but nevertheless, I did have episodes of stumbling. I sensed the Lord telling me I would have to keep my part of the covenant (the one between me and God), if I expected Him to work a miracle in restoring our home. My determination to win kept me in check as my flesh wrestled with the Holy Spirit of God, who lived on the inside of me. It reminded me of Jacob wrestling with the Angel of the Lord. When the fight was over, he was called Israel, meaning, "He that striveth with God." When my fight was over, I would be called Deborah Ross—"the one who strove with God to overcome marital adversity."

> *And he said, Thy name shall be called no more Jacob, but Israel: for as a prince hast thou power with God and with men, and hast prevailed.*
> —GENESIS 32:28

My husband and I went to Christian counseling together—
as well as separately—over the next eight weeks. This pastor
(the same one I saw the first day I collapsed in the lobby of
our church office) was instrumental in the salvation of our
marriage. He spoke to my husband like a daddy, sometimes
gently leading and sometimes rebuking. For the most part, he
was very gentle with me, acting as a mediator between us but
leaning toward helping my husband to understand the need
for doing "whatever I said," for a season.

- I needed my husband to prove his determination
  to win back my affection.

- He needed to convince me that I was the most
  beautiful woman he had ever seen.

- Sincere repentance over his past lifestyle needed
  to be humbly pouring from his mouth—every
  second of every minute.

- He needed to tell me, "Thoughts of ever
  being with another woman, other than you, is
  nauseating."

- I needed him to tell me he loved me—over and
  over and over and over, again and again.

This preacher knew it would take a lot of work for my
husband to earn my trust, and he helped me to articulate my

feelings, oftentimes serving as a man-to-man interpreter to my husband. He would say things like, "What she is saying is..."

My counseling instructions were, "You must forgive your husband. Forgiveness is a commandment, not an option." I was not, however, told I must stay married to my husband. Staying married after infidelity was a choice God would let me make on my own, but I figured, "If I must forgive my husband, I might as well stay married to him!" It seemed like too burdensome a task to forgive him and then not receive the prize for my hard work. In my mind, forgiveness and divorce were an oxymoron; I couldn't imagine forgiving the love of my life and then handing him over to marry someone else!

> *And when ye stand praying, forgive, if ye have ought against any: that your Father also which is in heaven may forgive you your trespasses. But if ye do not forgive, neither will your Father which is in heaven forgive your trespasses.*
>
> —Mark 11:25–26

In the past, I had always found it easy to forgive people; however, up until this point, I had never been put in a situation that required me to forgive torrential offenses hailing from so many sources all at once. God's requirement seemed too enormous for my mind to conceive. I did not want my Lord to hold me accountable for my past sins—which were many—so I knew I must figure out a way to forgive every person who hurt me during this trial, regardless of whether their wounds were inflicted by ignorance or malice. But how?

Overwhelmed by the task of forgiving so many people all at once (my husband, the adulteress, our relative, myself, and even God), coupled with the fact that our financial situation appeared to be hopeless, I found it hard to cope. In one of our counseling sessions I was taught something that saved me from mental breakdown, and I pray in sharing it, many of you will find relief in your situation. My pastor said:

- I should compartmentalize each overbearing thought.

- Then, he said I should prioritize each task; concentrating on one task at a time, leaving the others in God's hands—until I was ready to deal with them.

With this advice, I was able to only concern myself with forgiving my husband. I continued to work in corporate America, but I did not worry about the future of our finances. I did not try to forgive the adulteress, my relative, or myself—yet.

About forgiving God: I prayed to Him every minute of every day, crying out, reminding Him of His Word, and binding Satan. I was striving with God and holding onto my miracle. I was real with God. My prayer time was passionate, loud, persistent, violent (against darkness), and bold. Like Jacob, I was not going to let go of God's Word until He blessed me!

And he said, Let me go, for the day breaketh. And he said, I will not let thee go, except thou bless me.
—GENESIS 32:26

During the first three months of our restoration period I continued working at my corporate job—although I absolutely hated it! Even though our marriage was in the process of being mended, there was still a need for me to earn a big salary because our finances were in such a wreck. Honestly, the more I worked, the angrier I became. My argument was, "Why should I have to dig us out of this ditch? I wasn't the one who got us into this mess in the first place!" Our counselor helped me to rationalize the need to continue working (for a season), but I didn't like it! Not one little bit.

Then, as expected, my boss sent me to Cincinnati one weekend. Coincidentally, my husband's boss sent him to Detroit that same weekend! Frustrated, I wondered, "Was God testing me...in the middle of a test?" It was a big enough challenge for me to forgive, forget, heal, and believe for better days, without the arduous addition of separation. In agony I thought, "How could I ever trust my husband to be away from home for a weekend; to have free reign in a big city—all alone? Would he drink? Would he flirt? Would he act like a Christian or a sinner?" The thought of trying to uphold a professional image at my job, while surviving an entire weekend of intense grief was like someone pouring gas on a forest fire. My mind went out of control. This weekend of isolation almost drove me over the edge.

When I returned home from Cincinnati, I was mad at God! I had a nasty attitude thinking, "How does God expect me to heal, forgive, and forget; yet, He doesn't give me time to catch my breath?" My life was a marathon of heartbreak, and it seemed God had no sympathy for my exhaustion. As my husband and I returned to counseling that next week, my apathetic attitude alarmed our pastor. For the first time in all of this ugly mess, I was mad at God! I wasn't sure I wanted to continue fighting for my marriage. After all, how could I expect to win, if God were not on my side?

On this day, my countenance was obviously a shock to our counseling pastor. Looking just like Cain before he slew Abel, I had a haughty demeanor (Genesis 4). I felt as though I had sacrificed everything in my power, and still, God was requiring more of me. The defining moment of Cain's bad character was revealed when he got mad at God. If I did not get control over my flesh, sin would rule over me in this same way. Would I kill our marriage, the way Cain slew Abel? As revealed in the countenance of Cain, sin was lying at the door of my heart, and I needed to change my attitude—fast—before I made devastating life-altering mistakes.

> *If thou doest well, shalt thou not be accepted? and if thou doest not well, sin lieth at the door. And unto thee shall be his desire, and thou shall rule over him.*
> —GENESIS 4:7

The preacher's response to me on that day was one I didn't want to hear—and one I'll never forget. He said, "You know, if you give up now, since you and your husband have reconciled sexually, you'll be the one committing adultery, if you decide to remarry." These words made me furious! I didn't choose this nightmare; it was given to me! And now, was this man telling me that it would be my fault, if I bailed out? Whoa! Even though I didn't like the message, it sure made me think. That preacher knew my allegiance was to a Holy God. I think he knew what my response would be, even before he made that comment. After thinking long and hard about his words that day, I repented of my anger. That same day, I made a decision to step out in faith, believing God for our finances in a big way. I quit my corporate job!

My prayer was, "Lord, I believe it is not Your will for me to continue to go out of town each weekend for work. I don't believe that you had me sell a twenty-year business—of which I enjoyed—only to leave me to function in a job that I despise. I surrender. I will not try to fix this problem myself. Help us, oh, God! Bless my husband. Give him favor to be the breadwinner of our home." This prayer was the beginning of a shift—from one that always focused on me, to prayers of God blessing my husband. It's hard to pray for someone you hate, and I found that as I prayed God's favor down upon my husband, God began to take my bitterness away. Hallelujah!

> *Bless them that curse you, and pray for them which despitefully use you.*
>
> —LUKE 6:28

> *Confess your faults one to another, and pray for one another, that ye may be healed.*
>
> — JAMES 5:16

I learned so much about the kingdom of God through my marital trials: forgiveness, perseverance, self-control, the power of mustard-seed faith, the faithful provision of God, and so much more. I'd like to share some of these things with you, praying you will be empowered to press on—winning the battle in your life.

Up until this point in my life, I had always thought of forgiveness as a "decisive moment." If someone did me wrong, I made a decision to forgive them, and that was that. Well, when the person who betrays you is someone that you deeply love and trust, such as your husband, the roots of bitterness grow much deeper. I quickly realized that the deeper the love, the more severe the injury; consequently, the harder it is to forgive. At first I said, "I'll forgive, but I'll never forget!"—not realizing that forgetting is a requirement for forgiving. What I was really saying was, "I will forgive, but only until something reminds me of the offense. In that case, I reserve the right to hate again." I had so much to learn.

Thankfully, one thing I was able to recognize almost immediately was the power bitterness had over my soul. I wanted to be soft and beautiful, not hard and ugly. My motivation for ridding myself of bitterness not only included pleasing God, but also encompassed a little vanity. I wanted to be beautiful!

Have you ever seen a bitter woman? There is nothing soft and beautiful about her. Her face is prematurely aged. Her presence is overbearing. Her countenance is sad and depressing. Very plainly said, "She is hard and ugly." I did not want to be that way. I wanted to grow old like my ninety-two year old grandmother who, although she has experienced more than her share of heartache and disappointment, still looks joyful, soft, full of life...and beautiful! I love make-up, high heels, beautiful clothes, smiles, and laughter, but the bitterness that was overshadowing me was robbing me of my entire existence.

Another motivational reason for my desire to purge bitterness was my health. I had watched my dad die of cancer ten years earlier, and now the devil was telling me that I had cancer. Bitterness was my cancer! I could literally feel the cells in my body rebelling. This bitterness in my soul was a seed sent from Satan to kill me! It had to be uprooted—out of the soil of my heart—or else Satan might claim the victory over my body prematurely, quenching the future plans God had for me on Earth. Oh, how I wanted to be freed from the poisonous drip of bitter thoughts, but how?

My counselor told me it might take just as long to heal my broken heart as it took to tear it apart. He was right—almost to the day. My husband was involved in an adulterous lifestyle for nearly nine months, and it took me over nine months to purge the bitterness that was destroying me. Some of you are wondering, "How did you purge yourself of bitterness? How could you ever forget what your husband did?" The answer is *prayer!*

Like child-birthing pains which are soon forgotten, God's grace and mercy, working through the power of the Holy Spirit in every Christian's life (who earnestly seeks to forgive) will erase painful memories. Today, I am free of all painful thoughts, bitterness, hopelessness, and fear. I have forgiven everyone who offended me throughout my life's journey, thus far, and on top of that God has replaced my anger with a heart of compassion—longing for those who offended me to know Jesus the way I do. Today, I have a great relationship with the relative who unknowingly hurt me. I can even say I have a sincere burden for the salvation of the adulterous woman who sought to destroy my home. I remind myself that I could have done these same things, under the right circumstances—had I not known Christ.

For all have sinned, and come short of the glory of God.

—ROMANS 3:23

Many of you are still asking, "But, how did you get to that place of forgiving and forgetting?" Let me take you back to my journey of forgiveness, sharing some revelations given to me from God, which may be helpful to you.

During my nine months of purging bitterness, healing, forgiving, and learning to trust again, I found out what a "prayer closet" really was. Up until this time in my Christian walk, I had always prayed beside my bed—usually during the day when I was alone in the house. Now, during these excruciatingly painful days of learning how to crucify the flesh, I found it was necessary to pray out loud—really loud—many times a day and, oftentimes, I even got up to pray in the middle of the night. During this season of my life, I would literally go to my closet and scream out to God, "Please take this bitterness from me!" I sobbed, "Take me up to the high place, so I can see my life from Your perspective. Lord, I am being crushed by the weight of my burdens. Please, put me on top of my problems!"

The LORD God is my strength, and he will make my feet like hinds' feet, and he will make me to walk upon mine high places.

—HABAKKUK 3:19

Although God would set me on high, helping me to make it through that day, the devil fought long and hard, trying to snatch my peace. Many sleepless nights, inundated by a river of tears, sent me into fight or flight panic attacks—as imaginative thoughts of my husband being with another woman ripped through my heart. It was during these times, I had to choose between beating my husband to death while he slept or running to our closet and crying out to God. Over and over and over again, I prayed the same prayer, "Lord, take me up to the high place. Help me to see my husband from Your perspective. Help me to forgive. Take these perverted thoughts out of my mind."

On many occasions, while driving my car, I would be overtaken by emotional outbursts of anger and rage. It was in those moments I had to make a choice of whether to receive those thoughts or to take them captive. The privacy of my car was a great prayer closet. I would get really loud, reminding God of His promises and recalling the many years of prayer in which I had lifted up my marriage to Him. I rebuked the devil, daring him to touch me or God's Word. I bound him and every demon I could name, claiming the promises of my God over every aspect of my life. These days of prayer were like none other. I had never encountered spiritual warfare like this before, but I was determined to fight my flesh and the devil's lies until I was made whole again. One of us had to lose and according to God's Word, it wasn't going to be me!

Casting down imaginations, and every high thing that exalteth itself against the knowledge of God, and bringing into captivity every thought to the obedience of Christ.
—2 CORINTHIANS 10:5

I learned more about the kingdom of God during these nine months than I had ever read about or heard preached in my entire thirteen years, since becoming a Christian. It was during this season of my life that God walked with me and talked with me in a way I had never imagined possible. Like Job, ever since I had become a born-again child of God, I had always believed God's Word, trusted Him, and worshiped Him. I considered myself to have great faith, never doubting the most radical of testimonies; but now, during my "mustard-seed" season of faith, I was living out His promises as—one by one—He would reveal stories in His Word that paralleled to my life. The Lord was engraining His truths into my heart and mind in a powerful way.

Our family experienced a supernatural encounter in the second month of our restoration process that I'd like to share with you in the close of this chapter.

One hot summer day, as our family headed out on a paddle-boat in the cove of a nearby lake, we encountered a supernatural manifestation of God's presence. It was not a windy day. In fact, there was no wind blowing at all, when suddenly, a whirlwind appeared. The surprising twenty-foot twister quickly funneled up lake water, spraying every member of our family with a refreshing burst of down-pouring rain. The blast was similar to the sprays made by slalom skiers who masterfully kick up beautiful fountains of water as they pass from side to side across the wake of a boat. As fast as this whirlwind came, it disappeared. Our entire family was drenched. We were stunned.

"Did you guys see what just happened?" I exclaimed to my family! Each of us knew something awesome had just taken place, but what was it? We knew it couldn't be our imaginations, because we were all soaking wet! Strangely, no one on the banks of the cove acted as though anything peculiar had even happened. It was as if the whirlwind was invisible to everyone but us. My husband and I could feel the presence of God, and we both believed that the Lord used His finger to stir the waters of that cove, baptizing us—as a family. God washed us clean! WOW!

Later that night, the Lord guided me to the precise scriptures, which paralleled the events of our day at the lake. As I read Job, chapter 38, I was amazed to hear what God was saying to my heart. The Lord pointed out to me how He had spoken to Job through the whirlwind. This is what He told me, "Deborah, the message I gave to Job is the same Word I am speaking to you. Now, listen to the meaning of why I manifested my presence today...and then obey my commands." As I studied this passage of scripture, the Lord gave me a strong rebuke, expecting me to heed His Word and claim healing for my soul.

You see, I had prayed twelve long years for my husband to become a born-again man of God, and now that he had given his heart to Christ, I didn't like the way that his salvation experience had transpired. I never thought I would be expected to endure the heartbreaking news of my husband cheating on me before my prayers could become reality. In my mind, because I had prayed for my marriage all those years, I expected it to be protected from the gut-wrenching pain that infidelity brings. If my husband would have become a born-again man of God sooner, I know that none of this would have ever had to happen. I certainly don't believe the Lord ever intended for my husband to go this far with his sin; however, since my husband never repented throughout the many trials we faced as a family, God allowed this dreadful act to take place, knowing that my husband would eventually cry out to Him for salvation.

In this life lesson, the Lord was teaching me through Job 38, to not concern myself with *how* He brought about salvation in the life of my husband, but rather to rejoice in the fact that He had, indeed, answered my prayer. Basically, the Lord was telling me to, "Get over it!" I'll admit, those were really strong words coming toward a hurting woman from her Lord, but you know what? They were the truth, and sometimes the truth hurts!

Then, the Lord took me to Ezekiel 36:25–38. He explained to me how He had washed my husband with clean water from heaven. There was no need for me to fear my husband ever doing the horrible things he had done in his past because God had given him a new heart. God promised me in verse 27 that He had put His Spirit into my husband, and His Spirit would help my husband to live a holy life from now on. My precious Lord even went on to tell me of how He would take away our financial problems. In verse 30, He said He would increase my husband's income so we would not be embarrassed by the heathen. As I questioned whether or not we "deserved" to be delivered from our financial disaster, God reminded me in verse 32 that He was not doing this for my husband's sake, but for His name's sake.

God's Words were like salve applied to an open wound...music to my ears...rest to my soul! My Lord, the God of the universe, came down to Earth and personally baptized our family. Then, He spoke blessings over us and anointed our heads. This was a defining moment in the journey of the Ross family. We were forever transformed, setting our minds like flint to believe nothing would be impossible for us. We were determined to rise above our circumstances, knowing God had appointed us to do just that. Even though our financial future looked bleak, we were confident that God would turn things around—we would not be ashamed! Hallelujah! Glory to God! Thank you, Jesus!

My husband is not an artist and has never drawn anything

throughout our entire marriage, but, on the night of our revelation (through God's Word) of the whirlwind encounter, my husband picked up a pencil and drew a picture of our experience with God on the lake that day. I'd like to share it with you...

CAne creek

LIFE APPLICATION

God wants to bless you and your family. Read Deuteronomy 28:1–14 to discover what God's blessing includes. Do you see the stipulation for receiving the fullness of God's promises? Ask God to help you pray these blessings over your spouse.

ten

GOD LOOKS AT THE HEART

LIFE LESSONS

- Check your motive(s). More than saving your family, God wants you to trust Him with a pure heart.
- Pray for God's Wisdom. Don't listen to the world's advice on how to have a good marriage.
- Obey the Holy Spirit. Only God can show you your pathway to victory.

The grace of our Lord Jesus Christ be with you all. Amen.

—REVELATION 22:21

I N WRITING THIS book, I have spent many hours on my knees, asking God to help me articulate my story—with His anointing—for the purpose of saving countless marriages from the curse of divorce. Throughout this process and upon years of ministry, I have begun to recognize a pattern of error made by numerous wives—all desperate in their quest for restoration with their spouse. While every person's story is a little different in how the road bends, God's Word remains the same for all, and the pattern of error that I have noticed among so many could very well be the deciding factor as to why some Christian women obtain the victory and some do not. I believe the answer can be found in the way each person responds to—and applies—the Word of God throughout their journey. Remember, God's Word is holy and must be handled according to His standards.

In thinking of an account from 2 Samuel 6, where Uzzah mishandled the ark of God, and was struck dead for his mistake, I am reminded of how our good intentions are not what God desires. While Uzzah meant well, by helping to cart the ark of God from the house of Abinadab to the city of David, he failed to adhere to the importance of God's require-ment in "handling" His presence. (The ark of God was to be carried on the shoulders of the priest, not on carts.) Tragically, when the oxen stumbled and Uzzah touched the ark to keep it from falling, his well-meaning deed was in error to the specific instructions God had given on how the ark was to be handled. It seemed like such a small mistake (a little thing), yet failure to pay close attention to detail meant death for Uzzah.

> *Behold, to obey is better than sacrifice, and to hearken than the fat of rams.*
> —1 SAMUEL 15:22

My exhortation to every hurting soul who seeks a God-centered family (a marriage made in heaven) is to keep in mind how the "little things" are consequential in the building-up or tearing-down of a home. For it is only by the sum total of each little step of faith and each small deed of Christlike love that Christians can expect wholeness in their marriage. Step-by-step and precept-upon-precept, the victorious Christian understands the importance of living out Christ before their mate. Though the enemy may cause emotions to run wild, the overcomer will be resolute in keeping a clean heart and a Christlike demeanor as they face their daily trials. God is not looking for perfect people, but He is looking for those who have a desire to be holy—because He is holy!

If we fight against our own cause, no matter how we justify it, God's Word will not work. That's like willfully committing murder and then asking God to bring the person back to life. Or, like foolishly jumping off of a hundred-story building and asking God to keep you from hitting the ground. Likewise, we should not expect God to restore our marriage when we ourselves are not willing to crucify our flesh by placing our emotions on the back burner long enough to act according to the Word of God. Our covenant with our heavenly Father has a prerequisite that must be adhered to in order for His Word to work effectively in our lives.

> *Every kingdom divided against itself is brought to deso-lation; and every city or house divided against itself shall not stand.*
>
> —MATTHEW 12:25

I believe the key to victory lies in these three fundamental conditions:

+ The method of application

+ The wisdom of timing

+ Our obedience to the Holy Spirit

Let's take a closer look at each of these three "keys" for a better understanding of what I mean.

METHOD OF APPLICATION

More than anything, God desires for us to know Him and to walk in fellowship with Him. If our only concern is to have a reconciled marriage, without a sincere desire to commit every aspect of our lives to biblical standards, regardless of our outcome, we are missing the mark. I have seen many carnal Christians who try to twist the arm of a righteous God with confessions of justified, rationalized, and downright selfish claims of faith. These women are only seeking to use God's Word as a means to their cause. Usually motivated by fear rather than faith, these distraught wives also refuse to submit to authority—the authority of God's Word, leaders of the church, elders, and the voice of the Holy Spirit.

The method used in applying God's Word to everyday circumstances can be the bridge that joins a life of despair with the road to victory. Apart from a pure motive, there are no words, nor any deeds, that are good enough to change the Lord's just requirement for obtaining His abundant blessings. When the method for which one applies God's Word is fueled by vain or disobedient motives, that person has created a breech in his or her covenant with the Lord. In this case, He has no obligation to move on their behalf. Failing to seek God with a humble heart is a mute point. The faith of a believer must be pure and simple—aiming only to please the Lord in every way—knowing He rewards those who "diligently" seek, trust, obey, and serve Him.

> *But without faith it is impossible to please him: for he that cometh to God must believe that he is, and that **he is a rewarder of them who diligently seek him**.*
> —HEBREWS 11:6, EMPHASIS ADDED

WISDOM OF TIMING

> *Wisdom is the principle thing; therefore get wisdom: and with all thy getting get understanding.*
> —PROVERBS 4:7

During my last year of suffering, I stayed in the book of Proverbs, crying out to God for wisdom, knowledge, and understanding daily. Solomon says, his father, David, taught him to get these three things if he wanted to be successful. Feeling as though my life were a failure, I was determined to find out how to obtain these three attributes God reveres as being essential for living the victorious Christian life. I wondered, "What is wisdom? Is it intellect, a college degree, someone's IQ, intuition, or common sense? Whatever it is, I sure hope God helps me find it!"

While pondering the book of Proverbs, chapters 1 and 2, I discovered God wanted me to seek wisdom, knowledge, and understanding as if I were searching for a hidden treasure; earnestly pursuing precious truths from God's Word that would guide me in all of life's trials. As I continued on in my study of how to get wisdom, I noticed God referring to Himself as "being" wisdom. After months of digging for a clearer understanding of what God was saying to me about wisdom, I concluded, *"Wisdom is found only in God's Word."* The world and all of its knowledge cannot bring success unless God's wisdom (the ability to discern or judge what is true, right, or lasting) takes precedence over all intellect.

While Solomon tells us wisdom is the principle (most important) thing, he also stresses the significance of getting understanding. If we expect wisdom to benefit our life, as God has declared, we must link wisdom to our understanding. Simply reading and knowing God's Word is not enough. When it comes to obtaining the abundant blessings our heavenly father has in store for us, we must understand how to *apply* truths from God's Word to our everyday lives.

> *That the God of our Lord Jesus Christ, the Father of glory, may give unto you the spirit of wisdom and revelation in the knowledge of him: The eyes of your understanding being enlightened: that ye may know what is the hope of his calling, and what the riches of the glory of his inheritance in the saints.*
>
> —EPHESIANS 1:17–18

OBEDIENCE TO THE HOLY SPIRIT

God's Word, coupled with faith and surrounded by patience, never fails. That is why it is imperative for those who believe God to restore their marriage carefully obey the voice of the Holy Spirit—at each defining moment throughout their journey.

I am bombarded almost weekly by the cries of hurting women, who all ask me the same questions and make the same statements. Perhaps you are also wondering:

- "What should I do when he does _____?"

- "Maybe I should just get on with my life and find someone else."

- "I tried that, but it didn't work."

- "How long will it take for my marriage to be restored?"

Below, I have broken each of these valid questions and statements down into headings, to enlighten your heart from God's perspective.

"WHAT SHOULD I DO WHEN HE DOES _____?"

While I can tell you what I did, or what I would do, only God can show you the pathway for restoration in your particular situation. God knows the road that leads to salvation. As believers, our job is to stay on course by carefully following the leading of the Holy Spirit. God the Father, the Son, and the Holy Spirit are the only ones who know what is beyond each of life's twists and turns. The Holy Spirit (who dwells in every born-again child of God) will tell you what should be said or done this week; then again, He may change His instructions completely for the next week. (Of course, admonition from the Holy Spirit will always be in line with God's Word.)

"Maybe I should just get on with my life and find someone else."

It grieves me when Christian counselors give advice to people in a marital crisis according to the "pleasing of their flesh." So often, I hear of someone having marital problems being told to get on with their life. Many counselors will say, "God wouldn't have you in this much distress." The fact of the matter is that God may be molding and shaping *you* just as much as He is seeking to save your husband. When God's people prematurely bail out of circumstances, to please their own flesh, God usually allows them to go through that same type of trial again and again, until they learn to be more like Jesus. Maybe that is why so many divorced people remarry multiple times. Perhaps they haven't learned to crucify the flesh, so history repeats itself, as God gives them yet another chance to "get it right." Sadly, many who never learn to do things God's way end up only to be bitter, often settling for a life of unfulfilled joy.

This reminds me of the Israelites as they traveled in circles through the wilderness for forty years. All they had to do was to obey God and boldly take over the Promised Land, but instead, they whined and complained; they listened to the voice of their flesh rather than the voice of the Holy Spirit, because they were afraid to persevere. In their minds, it was easier to eat manna and quail in the desert, than to conquer the giants of the Promised Land—to eat choice fruits and vegetables. Yes, God was with them. After all, He's the one who provided the manna and quail for them to eat, even in their disobedience. Yet, this was not God's best.

I pray everyone reading this book will draw a line in the sand and not back down from receiving the inheritance of God's best. God wants you to be with the husband (or wife) of your youth. Don't allow your flesh to rob you of the joys that can only be experienced in the Promised Land. Hold fast to your faith and obey the voice of the Holy Spirit! No counselor, friend, or relative can tell you exactly how to remedy your dilemma. That's the job of the Holy Spirit. Then, once the Lord gives you His direction (for a specific moment of crisis), patience must be exercised. Patience is usually the hardest part!

> *Let thy fountains be blessed: and rejoice with the wife of thy youth.*
>
> —Proverbs 5:18

"I tried that, but it didn't work."

Above all I pray you'll never say, "I tried that, but it didn't work." God did not ask you to try anything; instead, He has commanded you to purposely live your life in such a way that is well pleasing to Him. If something from God's Word does not work in my life, I like to examine myself rather than shake my fist at an all-powerful God. First and foremost, Christians need to reverence God in the fear of holiness. Once we have postured ourselves as understanding His ways are higher than our ways, and His thoughts are higher than our thoughts (Isaiah 53:9), then patience must be exercised with a meek and humble spirit, knowing our Daddy—Abba Father—loves us far more than anything we could ever comprehend in this human life. Victorious Christians wait patiently for God's Word to manifest with supernatural favor!

> *But the fruit of the Spirit is love, joy, peace, **longsuf-**
> **fering**, gentleness, goodness, faith, Meekness, temperance:*
> *against such there is no law.*
> —GALATIANS 5:22–23, EMPHASIS ADDED

"HOW LONG WILL IT TAKE FOR MY MARRIAGE TO BE RESTORED?"

I guess the most agonizing question everyone asks is, "How long will I have to wait for my miracle?" My answer is, "As long as it takes." True warriors don't quit, just because the battle is too long. They fight until the death. I am not saying that God requires us to die in battle. Not at all. What I am saying is, "We should be willing to die for the cause of Christ." This is especially true when it comes to leaving a legacy in the lives of our children and grandchildren.

> *And they overcame him by the blood of the Lamb, and*
> *by the word of their testimony; and they loved not their*
> *lives unto the death.*
> —REVELATION 12:11

Granted the choice is up to each individual; however, I believe, once a person becomes undaunted in their stance to fight until the end, it is in that precise moment that they have created fertile ground for God to step in and defy all of nature—touching their situation to instantly turn things around. When I was squeezed into a corner and the verdict was placed in my lap to choose between marriage and divorce, it was in the very moment that I chose to lay my life down for my husband, for the sake of my children, and the call of ministry on my life, that God changed my circumstances—forever.

God's people must learn to stand their ground when crisis and conflict arise. Crucifying the flesh is not fun. Many times, it will require laying down our own emotions, desires, comforts, dreams, and even visions. The good news is that when God raises us back up again, we are much happier, and the anointing of God on our lives is far greater than when we first started. Glory to God!

Recalling a childhood church song, "Be Careful Little Ears What You Hear," my exhortation is for those planning to overcome their marital problems to close their ears to so many voices. Acting on advice from the wrong source could be the deciding factor in whether or not God's people finish the race as "more than a conqueror" rather than as one who "died in the wilderness." Remember, "Iron sharpens iron," so glean from Christians who have a warring spirit. Never listen to the ideas of the heathen. And, only take instruction from the Holy Spirit. Who knows, your life may take on the same form as the company you keep!

In my opinion, someone who has never been through this type of hardship cannot fully relate to the turmoil of another. I always thought, "I would definitely leave a man who cheated on me," but once I was forced into a real-life test of my will, I found out that I had the strength (through the blood of Jesus) to stay married, even through infidelity. Having come from a broken home, I have seen both sides of the track. Let me tell you, the grass is not always greener on the other side. If we would learn to mow and manicure the grass we have, others would be looking at our yards with envy.

Today, my husband and I are that manicured yard. Our marriage is stronger than ever. We are passionately in love. We have joy and peace unspeakable! Thank You, Jesus!

Much to our surprise, once my heart was healed, and my husband proved his salvation—by living a life that hungered and thirsted for righteousness—God moved our family out of our Pentecostal church. Even more astonishing, He moved us back to the fast growing Baptist church we had once attended. We are still Pentecostal believers, but we have found that God's power and blessing flow among all His children who worship Him in Spirit and in truth. While I still hold fast to the awesome wonder of my prayer language and the benefits I receive from praying in the spirit regularly, I love my brothers and sisters in Christ who don't see eye-to-eye with me on spiritual gifts. Although I am still passionate in sharing biblical truths concerning the gift of tongues, as well as teaching God's Word on all of the spiritual gifts, I respect the settled hearts of those who have a great love for the Lord, yet feel they have no need for these gifts.

Ever since God worked a miracle in our family, we have been going from glory to glory, in every aspect of my story. God says

He will give us the desires of our heart (Psalm 37:4), and my life is living proof of this promise. Not only did I desire to have a born-again husband and a whole family, but I also had a deep yearning to live in the destiny God had prepared for me—some secret desires of my heart that only He could fully understand and make happen. God knows all about my inner longings for peace, success, financial stability, a life in ministry, visions coming to pass, and my hope of leaving a legacy. He knows all about those things that I consider too big for me to accomplish. Here again, my Lord has proven His love by allowing me to do and obtain things that I desire. He is promoting me—to just be ME! How liberating is that?

In addition, the Lord has slowly delivered us from our debts. It is still a miraculous wonder as to how we have overcome each hurdle of critical financial challenges throughout the years following my husband's salvation. One thing is for certain, God's Word is true, and His deliverance is sure! As close as we have come to financial ruin over the course of our journey, the Lord has never let us fall into a point of no return. He has been faithful to slowly restore our wealth.

Even throughout our season of "little by little" financial deliverance, the Lord has allowed us to go, as a family, on three foreign mission trips to Brazil. On top of that, He gave us a wonderful vacation in the Cayman Islands one year. As an added blessing, He has provided the resources for us to do some much-needed updates to our home—the one we almost lost in foreclosure. The God we serve is mindful of every aspect of our lives. As we seek to serve Him in all of our ways, He blesses us with the ability to live our lives "out loud." Certainly, God has done exceedingly and abundantly, above all I could ever ask or think, in causing His Word to come to pass throughout the hills and valleys of my life's journey. As I told you in the introduction, "What He did for me, He'll do for you...just believe!"

We don't know what God is doing behind the scenes of our conflicts. Our job is to obey the Holy Spirit and then leave the timing and results in God's hands. One thing is for sure, "A quitter never wins," but glory to God, "A winner never quits!" Now be blessed in your journey—because God loves you...and your family! Amen!

LIFE APPLICATION

Study the entire book of Proverbs to find wisdom, knowledge, and understanding for your situation. Study the book of Psalms to find peace for your soul.

Having done all—*stand* (Ephesians 6:13).

MARRIAGE PRAYER

Remnant Women Bible Studies

Dear God:

Help me to understand that I cannot change my husband. I can only change me!

Help me to have faith knowing that You can change my husband.

Lord, help me to be more like You toward my husband, so that Your love will convince him of Your presence, Your power, Your kingdom principles, and Your authority in our marriage. Help me to do him good and not evil all the days of my life. I pray his heart will trust in me (Proverbs 31:11–12).

May he be won unto salvation by my meekness in Christ Jesus. May he grow in Christ to become all that you have called him to become.

Lord, you ordained families and set them in order according to your wisdom. Empower me to be a helpmeet (Genesis 2:18). Teach me to compliment my husband and offer daily assistance toward my husband's dreams, goals, desires, and plans. Help me to be at peace under my husband's rightful place as head of our household. I know that You will take care of me, as I do my part by giving honor to my husband (even while he is a sinner or I disagree with his choices).

I will not forsake the truth, but I will always apply the truth in a loving way so that your glory shines through my convictions.

Help me to love my husband at all times, even when I feel that he doesn't deserve my love. Help me to be intimate with my husband.

I pray that the blood of Jesus will cover my marriage and cause our family to flourish as an example to the world.

In Jesus' name, amen.

BECOME A CHRISTIAN!

Accepting Jesus as Your Lord and Savior

(READ JOHN 3 BEFORE PRAYING THIS PRAYER.)

ACCORDING TO SCRIPTURE, you must be born again in order to enter the kingdom of God. Romans 10:9–10 (KJV) says:

> *That if thou shalt confess with thy mouth the Lord Jesus, and shalt believe in thine heart that God hath raised him from the dead, thou shalt be saved. For with the heart man believeth unto righteousness; and with the mouth confession is made unto salvation.*

By repenting of your sinful lifestyle, sinful ways, pride, and self-centeredness, and by trusting the God of the universe to wash you clean, you can pray this simple prayer and expect God to make you one of His children...a new creature in Christ!

Then, after you have prayed this prayer, you need to tell someone what you did. It is by the confession of your mouth that your born-again transformation is complete, according to Romans 10:9–10. (Be sure to let me know about your born-again experience!)

Make these words your own as you pray:

Dear Lord,

I repent of my sinful behavior, my sinful lifestyle, my anger, my pride, my self-centeredness, my _____, and come to You humbly, asking for Your forgiveness. I believe that Jesus is the Son of God, who came to Earth to be crucified, buried, and raised from the dead.

Even though I might not fully understand how my accepting Jesus makes me a born-again Christian at this point, I am convinced that I am a sinner in need of a Savior, and I believe by faith that Jesus is the way to the Father. I am putting my trust in Your word by making Jesus my Lord and Savior, right now.

Please wash me clean. Cause me to hunger and thirst for Your word. Open my eyes that I might be able to understand the Bible. Take my life and mold it into the perfect destiny that You had in mind for me before the foundations of the world. I love You. I believe in You. I trust You.

In Jesus' name, amen.

Let me know of your decision!